*Dedication:*

*To Paul, Sarah and David. Unique vessels in the hand of The Creator; born to transform the lives of many.*

# BECOMING eXTRAORDINARY

## DR. GODWIN UDE

iUniverse, Inc.
Bloomington

# BECOMING EXTRAORDINARY

iUniverse books may be ordered through booksellers or by contacting:

iUniverse
1663 Liberty Drive
Bloomington, IN 47403
www.iuniverse.com
1-800-Authors (1-800-288-4677)

ISBN: 978-1-4759-6493-6 (sc)
ISBN: 978-1-4759-6495-0 (hc)
ISBN: 978-1-4759-6494-3 (ebk)

Library of Congress Control Number: 2012923125

Printed in the United States of America

iUniverse rev. date: 01/08/2013

Scriprures Refernces: King James Version

# Contents

# Introduction

The ordinary life is a life operating below God's purposes and plans. Mediocrity can be both a curse and a consequence. It is sad to realize that some of those who have been renewed in Christ as stars have slid down into the miry clay of life because of ignorance. Consequently, life has become a game of trials and struggles for these people. This book explores some of the reasons for such disappointing shows in life by believers. It is important to understand that God, who is the author of all humans, has no favorite gender, race, or age group. Of course, God also has no grandchildren. Every man was conceived during the fertilization of an ovum by a sperm cell, and most stayed in the womb through the nine months of the normal human gestation period, during which all they needed to excel in life was endowed upon them by God. This agrees with my accepted principle of divine design, which state that "every man is a product of definite design by God, perfectly suited for a particular assignment, and this is enhanced by his physical, spiritual, and emotional components." This means that no one is a product of biological accident or the outcome of a long-term evolutionary trend. The simple truth is that God has no time to create a Mr. Mediocre, and I feel it is a gross disappointment to God for anyone to settle for anything short of excellence in life.

Natural birth, which obviously happens for each living person despite the odds of millions of cells, means that every person alive on earth today became a winner right from the womb. There were about five million spermatozoa that contested for the egg that would become you, but one sperm cell saw the egg and took off in hot pursuit, and by supernatural maneuverings made possible by the power of the Holy Spirit, you made it to this earth as a unique human being with coded divine instructions for a purposeful life.

Having experienced the change that results when one decides to reorient his belief system and begins to pursue excellence in life by appropriating his divine privileges and opportunities innately built in him by God, I was motivated to put these discoveries down in book form.

I believe that no matter what the challenges of life may be, no believer should surrender his life to fate. We are children of purpose and must live as such. Situations do not determine us; we determine situations by how we react to them.

What you have in your hand is the revealed and well-articulated prescription for your emancipation. I believe that the careful study and assimilation of the teachings in this book will impart to you the required escape velocity you have long waited for. I offer this book to you with love as my humble contribution in your quest to maximize your potential and actualize your dreams in life.

This book is also especially packaged for those who are not satisfied with the status quo called ordinary! This is not a mere philosophical or religious thesis expounding some fundamental doctrines. This is the life story of a young man who rose from obscurity to become a Christian scholar and practitioner who led many Christian organizations. This book is both motivational and inspirational.

This is my story. I believe that sharing what helped me and still helps me accomplish God's purpose for me is the best way I can show my appreciation to God for what He did and is still doing in my life.

This book contains short chapters, each beginning with a quotation and a verse of the Bible. The body text of the chapters contains challenging sentences that have the power to cause anyone to rethink his position on the topic being discussed.

Teachings from this manuscript have been delivered in conferences on three continents and in many churches across Canada, Europe, and Africa. I have also shared the teachings with my online group subscribers and friends. The results have been astounding!

# Chapter 1

## Understand Your Peculiarity

*Before I formed you in the womb I knew you, and before you were born I consecrated you; I have appointed you a prophet to the nations.*

Jeremiah 1:5 (NASB)

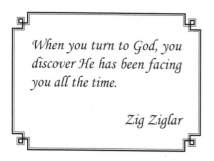

*When you turn to God, you discover He has been facing you all the time.*

*Zig Ziglar*

Nobody is the product of a biological accident. If you think you were born without an ordained purpose and plan, then you need to have a rethink now. God has no time to create a failure, a nonentity, or a mediocrity. He has a purpose for whatever He does.

When He created man and put him in Eden, He had a purpose. "And God said let us make man in our image after our likeness: and let him have dominion over the fish of the sea, and over the fowl of the air, and over the cattle, and over all the earth, and over every creeping thing that creepeth upon the earth" (Genesis 1:26).

You were created to have dominion; you were born as a king over a kingdom, extending from the Arctic to the Antarctic. You were created to *manage* the whole universe—a kingdom with limitless

1

expanse. You were created to be a master over the birds, demons, witches, wizards, and all the forces of the air. You were created to rule over the fishes, demons, forces, marine spirits, and every other created thing in the seas, oceans, and rivers. Friend, you are not a Mr. Nobody but a Master of the Universe.

Can you imagine being selected out of millions of "persons" struggling with you to be conceived in your mother's womb? God picked you up, called you forth, breathed His life into you, and deposited in you His creative ability, and what came forth after nine months of special preparation was you. What a wonderful you!

The prophet Jeremiah felt like so many of us. When God asked him to carry out his purpose for living, what he saw was a frail, weak, wimpy, shy, and incompetent boy. He felt he did not possess the stern and rugged countenance of other prophets. He looked so small and timid. He felt his colleagues would laugh at him when they learned he had become a preacher. He was scared of being his true self. He forgot that he didn't make himself. He thought he was a child of misfortune. No wonder he said, "Ah, Lord God! Behold I cannot speak: for I am a child" (Jeremiah 1:6).

It pains God when we place a question mark where God has placed a full stop. We often fail to consider from whom we came forth. Jeremiah forgot that God, who made him, did not forget to create his mouth properly for the job He was calling him to do. God cannot call a man to do what He has not prepared and equipped him for. Your abilities equal your responsibilities.

Let us look at another mediocrity turned Master of the Universe. The man Moses was a miracle baby. But God had planned Moses's life from conception. His birth, security, and training in the palace of Pharaoh revealed God's eternal ordination and subsequent preparation of Moses for his calling as a deliverer.

Despite all that Moses possessed—the wisdom and knowledge of the literature, arts, and sciences of Egypt, courtesy of his palace life—he complained of his speech impediment. It is obvious that man's limitation is often self-limitation. Anytime you decide to march off the map, you are ready to escape the ordinary. The ordinary life is the life of complaints and blame comprising, casting aspersions and accusations on people as the root of your problems.

Note today that you are created for a purpose. Be careful before your complaints breed constant pains to you. Understand that imitation can birth a life of limitations. Be different! Be yourself, and explore your God-given talents. Discover your peculiarity, for that is your comparative advantage. Never allow your seeming limitations to seal you off from your life visions and possibilities. One man with his God is greater than a multitude of great warriors without direction.

## A Personal Account

As a young teenager, I discovered I possessed great communication skills. I could hold a crowd with words anytime and anywhere, and I could do so effortlessly and smartly too, without feeling easily exhausted. In fact, my peers gave me a nickname for that, after a powerful talk-show music maestro. Many folks used to complain about my loquaciousness. Such comments troubled me so much that I asked the Lord to remove the spirit of loquaciousness from me. But the Lord did not answer me. He only gave me power and wisdom to control it and to communicate the truth of His Word. Little did I know that I have in abundance what the prophets Jeremiah and Moses complained they didn't have—yet God used them mightily.

Now, I believe that with the anointing of the Holy Spirit upon my life and my good communication skills, I can perform more excellently in my calling as a preacher/teacher than so many "Jeremiahs" and "Moseses" who retort and complain that they can't talk because of fear.

Oftentimes, what you complain about as a major fault in your life may be God's deposit for your breaking through the realm of ordinary into the realm of extraordinary. It may be your family background, height, complexion, other physical features, or even your family members. Discover your distinctiveness today and become extraordinary.

Whatever you complain about, you cannot change. Whatever you tolerate, you should not complain about.

Get ready for a change!

# Chapter 2

## You Are Born a Star

*There is one glory of the sun, and another glory of the moon, and another glory of the stars: for one star different from another star in glory.*

*1 Corinthians 15:41*

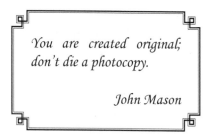

*You are created original; don't die a photocopy.*

*John Mason*

By virtue of your redemption, you now possess a rare combination of privileges. Firstly, you now have victory over the devil, who is the architect of sin, failure, confusion, and death. Secondly, you have been translated from the kingdom of darkness, failure, and mediocrity into the kingdom of light, success, and stardom.

Though born a star, you need to understand that you will not shine until the blood of Jesus refines you. There will be no twinkling for you until you are justified and glorified.

Stars are part of constellations, yet they are distinct among themselves. Their ability to twinkle lies in their distinctiveness. Many stars have further distinguished themselves with mobility and are thus referred to as shooting stars. You need not only shine; if you must escape the ordinary, you need to shoot and fire consistently within your chosen field or God-given vision in order to distinguish yourself from the crowd of stars and become a shooting star. You have to give birth to yourself if you must stand out in the world. Though born equal, we each have distinct deposits of talents, gifts, and skills required for a life of greatness embedded in us.

Avoid following the crowd. Be yourself! That's the best you can be. It is better to fail in originality than to succeed in imitation.

Limitation is the product of a life of imitation. Moreover, if you leave your own region to occupy another's, you will probably lose both regions and subsequently fail. Be yourself; you can never be anything else better. The sky is so vast; how can two birds collide? Collusion in life is a product of deviation from divine purpose. Avoid crashing out of life as a result of unnecessary competitive spirit.

Men who discovered their inherent potentials and applied them in solving the problems of humanity have made great world discoveries. If you can't walk except where you see another person's tracks, you will make no new discoveries for yourself. Do not follow where the path may lead; go instead where there is no path and leave a trail. Trailblazers are men with vision. Impact and dominion are two important impressions they leave behind on their journey to stardom.

You can't escape the ordinary life by trying to be what you know so well you are not. You must discover what you are created to be and pursue that with a consuming zeal.

Almost every man wastes part of his life in an attempt to display qualities he does not possess.

Don't let your life be a continual struggle by trying to be what you are not designed to be. You must not be everything, but you can be something.

If you must be something, then be the best of that thing to the praise and acknowledgment of your contemporaries.

You are like a tree; you must put forth the fruit that's created in you. Something is special about you that you do not know. I have a feeling in my spirit now that if you are willing to pursue it, your financial, mental, and spiritual breakthroughs will take place.

Nothing about you is common. Even the structure of your nose has its distinctiveness. No two fingerprints are the same. Don't you think that God who created you took time out to source His materials and assess, arrange, and analyze them before He formed you in a specifically designed mold? Has it ever occurred to you that whatever caused Jesus to forsake His glory and position in heaven to die for you is not a joke? You have no right to disappoint creation and ridicule salvation by accepting mediocrity as your fate. Get it right now! God has no time, and will have no time, to create Mr./Mrs./Miss Nobody or Chief Mediocrity. You must run from the ordinary life; it is a disappointment to God. Make the best use of what you have, and blaze a trail. Enter your world with big bangs of discoveries, inventions, and achievements.

You have a single life to live; make the best of it. Opportunities come several times, but the same opportunity may not repeat itself. Your breakthrough lies in your peculiarity and not in your similarity. You have no right to complain about what you permit. As author J. Oswald Sanders said, "Eyes that look are common. Eyes that see are rare."

Stardom is meant for stars and not mediocrities. Every man born of God is born a star. However, to get to stardom, you must twinkle consistently. Better still, you can shoot yourself into greatness by emitting lights of diverse but consistent frequencies.

"There is a path which no fowl knoweth, and which the vulture's eyes hath not seen; the lions whelps have not trodden it, nor the fierce lion passed by it" (Job 28:7–8). That secret path is still undiscovered, but I assure you today that you have the map with you now. Why not bend down and locate it. Once you discover it, don't trek or walk; rather, run and fly along that path as a shooting star. As my mother told me when I was a child, "Son, you can be all you want to be if you want to be all you want to be."

# Chapter 3

## Overcoming the "Auto" Problem

*You can't perform anytime more than you evaluate yourself at that time.*

*I can do all things through Christ which strengtheneth me.*

*Philippians 4:13*

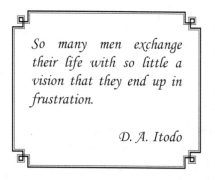

*So many men exchange their life with so little a vision that they end up in frustration.*

*D. A. Itodo*

Every man's problem can be located within the distance from the crown of his head to the base of his skull. Mental sickness is the worst sickness. People with mental illnesses suffer severely because no drug can effectively bring them to normalcy. When a man cannot assess himself to discover his potentials, he will end up in frustration.

Vision is a driver that pulls rather than pushes. Climbing the mountains of excellence can be difficult without a life vision.

The difference between winners and runners-up lies in the magnitude of their individual vision. While winners know and pursue excellence, runners-up doubt if their goals are possible.

Winners say, "It is possible," while the mediocre says, "It could be possible." Winners say, "What if it works out?" while ordinary men say, "What if it does not work out?"

A mediocre-minded individual is a dangerous person to befriend.

Research has shown that positive impacts are made in a working environment when positive and motivating words are discussed and shared freely in the workplace. Everyone believes in success, but only a few seem to have given it what it takes. The willingness is there, the desire is kindled, but the necessary motivation is lacking. This is because some individuals associate their failures with certain people or mystical powers and influences from so-called enemies. While these associations could be true, it is worth noting that no man has ever broken through in life without facing obstacles.

The fact that you have located some problems on your pathway to success demands that you gather yourself and face those problems squarely. By the anointing of the Holy Spirit, every curse upon your life is broken in Jesus's name.

Jesus Christ became *accursed* that you may partake of the blessings of Abraham. These Abrahamic blessings include long life, success, prosperity, good health, fruitfulness, righteousness, victory over challenges, and eternity. Anything short of these blessings is not God's wish for you and should not be accepted on any account. Sir William James pointed this out in this way: "The greatest discovery of my generation is that a human being can alter his life by altering his attitude."

Your thought life is a powerful part of you that rules your life. Your mind is located in the region of your soul, and this is the region of thoughts, emotions, will, and feelings. Your soul is accessible by various influences, both negative and positive. The unregenerate man may find it difficult to control the negative influential forces, and consequently, what he reaps is distorted and destroyed destiny. But the re-created man's spirit is re-created and empowered by the Holy Ghost to do good in the midst of the bad, to sift out the negative suggestions, and to obey the positive directives. The re-created man makes decisions based on revelations and not on suggestions. "Those who are led by the Spirit of God are called sons of God" (Romans 8:14).

The regenerated man has no excuse for his failures. It is an aberration to possess a re-created spirit, a renewed mentality (mind), and a reactivated body and still be a failure. Failure here means incomprehensible confusion and lethargy. Laziness and nonchalance are not part of our kingdom heritage. You can get there only if you say to yourself today, "I can." Your problem is located within, because you hold the key to your life. Anything that you allow in your life automatically rules your life. Men can allow what goes in and out of their lives. There is no way you will escape the ordinary if you continue seeing yourself as an incapable, weak, and unfortunate person. You can be delivered from this piteous mentality in Jesus's name.

## The Irony of Jabez

Have you read the case of Jabez from the Scriptures? The Bible starts by saying that Jabez was more honorable than his brothers. With this initial statement, one may be tempted to conclude that Jabez must have been born with a silver spoon in his mouth. The Bible has a way of presenting an episode in a funny, sarcastic way. Reading further down in the same chapter (2 Chronicles 4:9–10) reveals a shocking condition: Jabez was born normal like his brothers, but his mother had inadvertently placed a curse on him by giving him the name Jabez. The mother probably wanted to use Jabez as a specimen to always remind herself that she suffered before giving birth to him. However, such gambling became dangerous, as Jabez (which means "sorrows") continued to encounter sorrowful conditions all his life. This serves as a reminder to be careful of the name you bear and what you call a thing or a person.

But soon a drastic revelation brought a revolution in Jabez's life. He felt an urge to stand up and declare his freedom. He was bent on escaping the ordinary. Then he remembered the God of Jacob—the God who changed Jacob (meaning "supplanter") to Israel (meaning "prince"). The Bible says he called on the God of Jacob and the God of Jacob answered him. When this happened, he who was born to be sorrowful became more honorable than his brethren.

I see God honoring you above your brethren and contemporaries in Jesus's name! Why not borrow a leaf from Jabez? Stand up and stand out. Don't let your past failures determine your future. Let everyone know you are up and out for a radical change.

You must make a conscious effort to run from ordinary life. The "auto" problem is the problem of self-limitation. This is because no one rises above his vision in life. I challenge you today to adjust your life for a ride toward stardom.

# Chapter 4

## Can a Lion Give Birth to a Goat?

*I have said, ye are gods; and beings all of you are children of the most high.*

*Psalm 82:6*

### Your Association Determines Your Acceleration

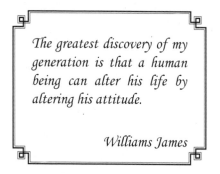

*The greatest discovery of my generation is that a human being can alter his life by altering his attitude.*

*Williams James*

There is a funny story about a goat born in the same house with puppies on a typical African farm. The puppies were called bingos, while goats were not often named. On several occasions, the farmer observed that each time he called the bingos, the goat responded alongside. Soon the goat started behaving like the bingos, to the extent that it started eating human excreta like the bingos. The farmer found that disgusting as well as amazing.

I believe some individuals can't live without trials because they keep on trying to be what they are not created to be. It is clear that trying to be like someone else is self-defeating. The main assignment everyone needs to pursue is to find out who he or she is and to give birth to himself or herself and not to another person. Faking is the act of limitation, while counterfeiting is the product of imitation. When imitation becomes a commitment, it gives birth to limitations in life and pursuits. If lions were to start giving birth to goats, the earth probably would change its orbit and axis. No genetic engineering will transform a lion to give birth to goats. This proves the fact that you are created to fully represent your creator and nothing less. "That which is born of the flesh is flesh: and that which is born of the spirit is spirit" (John 3:6).

God gave birth to Himself in you. Nothing was missing during the transfer. You are created to represent your creator fully, and to operate in His full power. By virtue of your new creation rights, you have become a re-created being in the Spirit. The evil nature, with its limitations, has been crucified with Jesus Christ. You have been given a brand-new spirit from God. You have been born again of God's Spirit, virtues, and power. As Christ rose from death and ascended to heaven, so you did rise from your damnable carnal nature to a glorified, powerful status in Christ, seated in heavenly places. By virtue of location, you are operating here on earth, but by virtue of position, you are seated in heavenly places with Christ Jesus. This means that you are an "above-only" person. That which is born of Spirit is Spirit. You are born of Spirit. If the spirit that raised Jesus Christ from the grave lives in you, it shall quicken your mortal bodies (see Romans 8:11). Yes! Your old nature has been transformed. You now have power with God. God has transformed Himself into you. He gave birth to Himself completely in you. The Spirit of God is God who is alive and active in you. No one carries the powers of a deity and lives an ordinary life. Go to a typical African village and ask elders; no witchdoctor goes about without an aura around him. Every witch doctor is revered and feared. Why? They all carry negative supernatural powers which are inferior to the power resident in every believer. You are greater than you think you are. Could God have re-created you to be subdued, intimidated, and frustrated?

Could God have left His exalted throne to die in order to raise nonentities and fearful men and women? What do you think about these things? If you are actually born of God, you have overcome the world. This is not contestable!

These are the words of Christ. You simply have to take charge till Christ comes back. Taking charge means being in control. Thus you must manage your resources and every affair; you must manage both your enemies and your friends.

Nothing should be out of control in your life. If you fail to occupy, then get ready to be occupied. If you fail to take charge, then you will be taken charge of. If you fail to be in control, then you will be controlled. You have to make you choice. You are a god—no contentions! Gods are dreaded and feared. They are called gods because they do some incredible things. You too can make things happen in Jesus's name. God gave birth to Himself when He gave birth to you. He did not make goats, fowls, and fish; He just called them into existence. He did not make the twenty-four elders, four beasts, and the hosts of angels; He called them forth (see Psalm 104). But God humbled Himself and took pains to literally give birth to Himself just like a woman spends time in the labor room to give birth to a child after nine months of pregnancy and preparation. Hence, you are not the child of a biological accident, nor are you a product of geographical dislocation. Right where you are, you are properly located to make maximum impact. Right at the very point you are at now, you have the most important thing it takes to escape the ordinary. Why not start now?

## Having Pleasure in Your Pressure

I was fortunately born into a large family with much pressure on the limited available food, clothing, shelter, and education. I was almost giving in to mediocrity when I encountered Christ and learned I was born a prophet to my generation. As I submitted to the guidance and direction of the Holy Spirit, I swiftly crossed over from the land of mediocrity to the land of mighty men. I was transformed from an ordinary life to an extraordinary one. I could not remain a natural man as supernatural manifestations took over. I assure you today that if you will only recognize the power of your re-creation, you will find out that you are here for a life of maximum impact. Don't settle for less, for you are a *god!*

# Chapter 5

## *Vision for Escape*

*Where there is no vision, the people perish. But he that keepeth the law, happy is he.*

*Proverbs 28:18*

*To be ahead is to see ahead. You cannot go faster than you see. The brighter you see, the faster you go.*

*David Oyedepo*

*If a man has no purpose for living, he is not fit to live.*

*Martin Luther King*

Everyone created by God and redeemed by His blood has a God-ordained purpose—an assignment or a task he is supposed to fulfill on earth. The mystery here is that even before you were born, God—by an act of predestination—had already chosen you and prepared a divine assignment for you. The Bible says in Romans 8:29-30, "For whom he did foreknow, he also did predestinate to be conformed to the image of His son, that he might be the first born among brethren. Moreover whom he did predestinate, them he also called: and whom he called, them he also justifies: and whom he justified, them he also glorified."

Now look at that wonderful sequence that ultimately leads to glorification. Each time I read the above passage, I try to figure out the particular level I am at, at that moment. But one thing is certain—I have not been glorified. Hence, like St. Paul, I press toward the mark for the prize of the high calling of God in Christ Jesus. At each level of life is a higher level. At any particular calling you answer, there is always a higher calling. I hear the voice of the Lord saying, "Break through to the next level. March off the map!"

Life becomes miserable without a focus. Vision introduces focus and flower to life. A visionless life is an actionless life. Such life ends in frustration. When your vision becomes your purpose and your purpose becomes your dream for life, then you are on your course for a life of stardom.

Vision has three vital functions that can elevate you to your zone of manifestations.

## 1. Vision Eradicates Waste

Vision is the cure for waste. Once you locate God's plan for your life and begin pursuing it, you won't want anybody to waste your time. In fact, the whole world steps aside for a man who knows where he is going. He is focused. If you are rushing to catch a flight and there before you is a visitor, what do you do? Of course you quickly excuse yourself and rush for your flight; otherwise, that journey will be cancelled.

Goals are definite points of action. Men of vision live waste-free lives because they have located their goals in life and have committed themselves to reaching those goals. You can never work on anything consistently without getting a result. The reason for many failures is inconsistency. You can't shoot at the corner away from the goalpost deliberately, unless you are not interested in victory.

## 2. Vision Infuses Energy

Confusion sets in when a man loses focus. This is followed by weakness and excuses. When you grow tired of an assignment, it is a sure sign that you are not pursuing your God-ordained vision. There is always an indescribable energy available to them who are rightly focused. This is because they have set before themselves success as the end. Having a bearing—something to direct your life and channel your spiritual and mental resources toward—is a major key to success. Without a bearing, life is bound to be boring.

## 3. Vision Enhances Focus

Distraction is the enemy of distinction. A company I know well uses this as their slogan: "No Distraction—That's Our Attraction." A force of attraction follows a man without distractions. This is because every wise man wants to associate with anybody that is focused. The Bible says that Jesus set His face as a flint (focused) toward Jerusalem for the final sacrifice that will liberate humanity from the hands of the devil. No wonder so many people followed him. They had confidence in Him. He commanded respect among the crowd—not just because of the miracles but also as a result of His composure, confidence, stability, and focus. The world has never produced a great leader who had no focus and yet succeeded as a leader. Focus brings with it a sense of direction, and direction enhances your acceleration.

You can break into the next level and escape the ordinary life swiftly by discovering and locating your vision for life. For every willing heart, God is always ready to reveal your life vision to you. "The secret things belong unto the Lord our God; but those things which are revealed belong unto us and to our children for ever, that we may do all the words of His law" (Deuteronomy 29:29).

Secondly, you have to discover your divine endowment or talents without consulting a spiritualist. You may be visibly manifesting a group of talents that, when properly harnessed, will bring about your liberation from many of your current problems. Why not pray through it and focus on it?

Thirdly, even if you think God has not shown you any vision and you have not discovered any indwelling talent, you must have a liking for something. This is your choice. I decided to be a pharmacist by choice. It is only through circumstance that it is related to my life pursuit and vision of helping people. Though God called me into the office of a prophet through several encounters, I could not make much impact as a minister of the gospel until I accepted the call from my heart. It became a choice, vision, and calling. When my calling was added to my indwelling talent of communication, I saw myself breaking through to new heights in the ministry. Guess what the secret is? You can hardly be mediocre at anything you commit your spirit, soul, and body to perform.

# Chapter 6

## Charge Your Mind

*Keep thy heart with all diligence: for out of it are the issues of life*

*Proverbs 4:23*

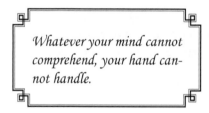

*Whatever your mind cannot comprehend, your hand cannot handle.*

The mind is undoubtedly the most active site in a man's life. It is the central processing unit (CPU) of life's "computer system." Every major discovery and breakthrough in any field of life can be traced to an active mind. Your mentality is the center of your creativity. It is important to note that nobody functions above his mental status. The more active your mental work, the more productive your handiwork and the more rewards you get.

Every change is traceable to a charge. No change occurs by chance. Situations and circumstances in your life may remain just as you want them. But you can change that unwanted pressure on your life with a charge right from inside your mind. When your mental status assumes the position of your desire in life, the forces of fortune will be provoked to respond to your desires.

Passion feeds the mind for swift productivity. The force of passion is the greatest weapon against frustration in life. Passion on your calling, talents, or choices potentiates your ascension to your dream's height. Never keep your mind idle, and never engage it on unworthy ventures. Another important factor for charging your mind rightly is the acquisition of relevant information. Information brings transformation. Every revolution at any historic time can be traced to a discovery and, subsequently, the acquisition of relevant information for that time of need. Your mind is an active consumer of information. Its principle of operation is the GIGO principle, which means "garbage in, garbage out." That is to say, you are what you think; and you can only expect a result akin to the type of information you feed into your mind. If you enjoy telling yourself how weak, feeble, and unworthy you are, then be prepared to live a weak, feeble, and unworthy life.

But it is a fact that if you inform your mind that you are able even in the midst of challenges and difficulties, your positive confession will bring about a positive altitude and, consequently, a life of success and excellence.

## The Battle Within

The battle on the mind is a fierce one because the devil has discovered its place in your destiny. Mentality is the greatest mold of destiny. Every destiny is either upheld or destroyed by the amount and type of information the mind receives and dwells on. Many lives have been ruined because the devil gained entrance into lives via the mind, thus hijacking and misdirecting activities along the lines of frustration and destruction (just like what [the human immunodeficiency virus—HIV] does to the immune system). The new creation is a privileged creation because it carries a Holy Ghost—refined mind. Notwithstanding, such a mind can be of no use until it is put to work. Your productivity is a function of your mentality. It is only a Holy Ghost—reconstructed mentality that can engage itself in a divinely directed, productive life. The secret of success lies not in any book written within or outside the country, but right within your mind.

When Dr. Napoleon Hill was on his success research assignment for Dr. Carnegie, he thought he was going to collate statistical facts and figures as the secrets for success. But to his surprise, among all the great millionaires and billionaires he interviewed and researched, he discovered one common denominator to their successes, and that was a charged mentality. It is interesting to note that most of these men were not born with silver spoons in their mouths. Amazingly, a great proportion of them rose from the Great Depression of the 1930s and 1940s in America to become celebrated successes.

Thus Dr. Hill propounded what is now referred to as Napoleon Hill's first law of success, which says, "What the mind of man can conceive and believe, it can achieve"

In other words, your achievement in life is a function of your mental status, and your mental status is a function of the amount and type of information you feed into it.

## Understanding Your In-Process Power

"Now unto him that is able to do exceedingly abundantly above all that we ask or think, according to the power that worketh in us" (Ephesians 3:20). I have confessed and applied this Scripture in my life several times. The word translated as "power" is the Greek word *dunamis*, which means "force that brings about a supernatural alteration." In other words, whenever God wants to suspend the natural in order to execute His plans in any life or situation, He applies dunamis. This force is principally released

Dr. Godwin Ude

to bring about a superlative transformational change beyond the comprehension of the ordinary mind. Now, imagine what such force can accomplish in your life when you allow God to take residence in your life.

Problems are only as unique as we believe them to be. With God, problems are simply divine assets, without which most destinies will remain subdued. It was a problem that transferred Joseph to his land of destiny without a visa. It was also a problem that launched him from prison to palace. It was a problem that announced the Davidic dynasty. It was the excruciating and humiliating sacrifice on the cross that redeemed humanity from the powers of sin, sickness, and poverty. God is not a victim of your problem, and you should not be one. The power resident in you as a believer is capable of demolishing every attack of the enemy against your life. Your assignment is to recognize this power and engage it to work for you.

At one time, I found myself in the wilderness of life, where hopelessness was the only oasis available for my thirsty soul. While praying, I heard God saying to me, "Son, beyond your dreams and expectations, I will lift you high." Since I discovered this power within, which is accessible by faith, I have prophesied the outcome of many challenges in my life. Friends, I believe that God intends the best for us. He is ever willing to take us beyond our expectations. Don't call that which you have never prayed about impossible. Remember, with God, all things are possible; even your present deplorable condition can be changed to your desired outcome by engaging this divine power within by faith confession.

Mentality is the greatest mold of destiny. To be spiritually mindless is death and frustration.

Reconstructed mentality brings about increased productivity. You are to be envied and not pitied. You can choose to be a liberator or a liability. The mind you have is the mind of God. The mind of God is a creative mind. You can therefore create your future by charging your mind.

# Chapter 7

## *Your Picture—Your Future*

*And Joseph dreamed a dream, and he told it his brethren: and they hated him yet the more. And he said unto them, hear, I pray you, this dream which I have dreamed: For, behold, we were binding sheaves in the field, and lo, my sheaf arose, and also stood upright and behold your sheaves stood and made obeisance to my sheaf.*

*Genesis 37:5–7*

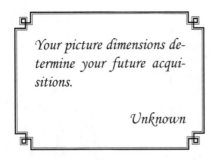

*Your picture dimensions determine your future acquisitions.*

*Unknown*

Your future is an open field waiting for cultivation. The amount of investment you put into it determines the result you will obtain. It is important to note that life does not respond to ordinary expectations; rather, it responds to your desires. However, desires are not the only bedrock of achievements, since the proof of desire is pursuit. A desire without pursuit ends in disaster.

The future holds so much for you. Command your desires into your future via the power of pictures. Your picture can be your future only when you convincingly convert it into power of vision for life. The devil understands the power of pictures. No wonder he has filled the minds of so many Christians with negative and black-and-white pictures. No wonder he has filled the lips of so many with negative confessions.

But you can halt such invasions from getting into your life. God has equipped you with His power and Word to command your desires into your future via the power of pictures. The life of Joseph is an example. From Scriptures, we understand that the young Joseph received a vision (referred to as a picture here). It was such a commonplace vision that some young and ambitious youths might delve in and out without giving serious thought to it. But we see Joseph with a zoom lens, magnifying his picture. He transformed the black-and-white, postcard-size personal picture into a well-framed, full-size, and colored life picture. With his confessions and declarations, he blew his pictures up to such dimensions that both his brothers and parents queried him.

While his brethren hated him and envied him, his father carefully observed him. "And he told it to his father and to his brethren and his father rebuked him and said unto him, what is this dream that thou hast dreamed? Shall I and thy mother and thy brethren indeed come to bow down ourselves to thee to the earth? And his brethren envied him but his father observed the saying" (Genesis 37:10–11). People with the proper picture of their future are objects of envy from their contemporaries. But envy is a tribute mediocrities pay to stars. The world steps aside for men that know where they are going. Until your picture becomes your daily obsession, it will not develop into your future.

Joseph's picture was a great one. His father could not contain it again; neither could his brethren. At one point, Joseph's father was convinced of the fact that his little boy was on a journey to greatness. Such a discovery should make a father happy, but the fact that even the father would in turn become one of Joseph's subjects made the old man ask, "Shall I and thy mother and

thy brethren indeed come to bow down ourselves to thee to the
earth?" What a question! But Joseph never said so. He was merely
relating his dreams, but in an obsessive manner. Joseph knew that
obsession is the mother of possession. The young man Joseph will
ever stand out as a man who knew how to transform his picture
into his future. Just an ordinary description of a dream made his
parents and brethren jittery. I pray that from this moment, your
dreams will result in your desired future in Jesus's name.

Every man is given the ability to dream, but not everybody has the
power of magnification and transformation, as Joseph had. This
is not because such abilities are not available to all, but because
not all are willing to explore these abilities. Thank God this book
presents to you, firsthand, the relevant information you need to
transform your obsession into your vision. If your dreams seem
impossible, then you are not exerting enough effort to force
them into real success. Talk it, say it, live it, walk it, stand it,
and picture it until you see it coming to pass. You must separate
yourself from the crowd. You can cease henceforth to be an echo
in the crowd, vibrating without distinction. There is still vacancy
on top; why not move into it? I must categorically state here that
the battle against mediocrity is a ferocious one. It involves your
spirit, soul, and body. Every step you take may be a deciding step
toward your desired future or away from your desired future. A
conscious effort should always be made to uphold the integrity of
your picture if you ever want it to become a reality.

The power of the picture was depicted dramatically well in
the life of Joseph. Right from the very moment he received
those revelations, his confessions and possessions of those
visions started. Even while in the midst of his brethren eating
and working, he was always seeing King Joseph. Right in the
pit, instead of crying, "Father, why hast thou forsaken me," he
was seeing Prime Minister Joseph Jacob. While as a servant in
the house of Portipher, he was seeing Prime Minister Joseph.
Inside the prison, where everybody wore gloomy faces, he was

bubbling cheerfully because he was always seeing His Excellency, Prime Minister Joseph Jacob, and not prisoner Joseph. It is not surprising that he finally reaped the fruits of his picture.

Acquisition of the right picture positions you for a drastic acceleration. No amount of intimidation or problems can overcome a man who has rightly pictured his future. Your picture must be constantly washed and redeveloped to standard in full color for it to meet the demand of the hour. From my adolescence, I have always had problems maintaining some friendships in which my friends were not comfortable with my obsessive dreams. You have to destroy all the encumbrances that will destroy your picture. *Capture it as you picture it!*

# Chapter 8

## *The Power Of Purpose*

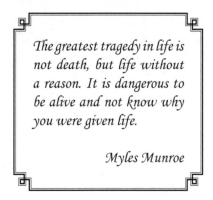

*The greatest tragedy in life is not death, but life without a reason. It is dangerous to be alive and not know why you were given life.*

*Myles Munroe*

"But Daniel purposed in his heart that he would not defile himself with the proportion of the king's meat, nor with the wine he drank: there he requested of the prince of the eunuch that might not defile himself . . . And in all matter of wisdom and understanding. That the king inquired of them, he found them [Daniel, Shedrach, Mishack, and Abednego] ten times better than all the magicians and astrologers that were in all his realm" (Daniel 1:8, 20 KJV).

The productive life is never an accident. It is simply a product of overtaking your limitations and weaknesses toward success in life. Life has no meaning without a clearly defined purpose. The deepest craving of the human spirit is to find a sense of significance and relevance. The search for relevance in life is the ultimate pursuit of man. Conscious or unconscious, admitted or not, this internal passion is what motivates and drives every human being, either directly or indirectly. It directs his decisions, controls his behavior, and dictates his responses to his environment.

No meaningful input can be used in life for a rewarding output until the purpose of existence is determined. This is a waste of time and effort when the wrong end is being pursued. Most men have worked hard but unfortunately have nothing to show for all their efforts. It is amazing to discover that the secret of success is not hard work but hard work with purpose. The ultimate desire of every life is to find fulfillment by achieving success, but fulfillment comes through a purposeful pursuit. Purpose is the key to life. Without purpose, life has no meaning. He who succeeds is not he who wakes up earliest, but he who keeps awake when it matters most. It is not the length of time spent but the quality of the time invested that matters. We have been told to continue in our hard work, but I encourage you to work hard *with purpose*. Life is meaningless without a sense of direction. Purpose is the power of your life, the reason for your living. Purpose is the problem you have been created to solve; the assignment, vision, and calling of God upon your life. Purpose brings focus, direction, and acceleration in life. Success is only achievable when purpose is discernible. Purpose is the master of motivation and the mother of commitment. Purpose is the common denominator that gives every creature a sense of destination. Vision provokes pursuit, and when your dream becomes your purpose, you are absolutely unstoppable. Until purpose is discovered, existence has no meaning, for purpose discovered is the beginning of fulfillment in life.

When there is no purpose, there is no self-control, no moral conviction, and no ethical boundaries. This is evident in both individual and corporate lives. When an individual does not find a reason for living, he begins to live mischievously. In the same vein, when a corporate body does not know why it exits, the organization fails, or it is adulterated or becomes an imitation. The glory of any life or organization is dependent on the defined and identified purpose of such a life or organization. Purpose gives relevance, identity, and definition. A defined life is a refined life.

The wave of crime in our society is a disturbing phenomenon. Most youths, sad to say, are perishing via crime because of a lack of purpose. Ask any young man on the street, "How is life?" and he will answer by saying, "We are trying." What a life of trial! Our leadership problem is the result of a loss of purpose. When purpose is lost, anything goes, including good, bad, and ugly. There is short-term thinking in society all geared toward immediate self-gratification. A lack of dreams, visions, and aspirations has resulted in many cut-and-join projects, which have kept the economies of some nations in limbo. Unfortunately, when society gropes in purposeless pursuits, people are constrained to follow suit. However, it is dependent on you as an individual to opt out and make relevant changes to your life, or you will drift away into oblivion because of your lack of purpose. It is important to note that your fulfillment in life is dependent on your becoming and doing what you were born to be and do. It is essential, vital, crucial, and necessary that you understand this fundamental principle of purpose and pursue it with all your heart, for without purpose, life has no heart. Never forget that those who don't know where they are going will probably end up somewhere else. But the world steps aside for someone who knows where he is going.

There is no excuse for your suboptimal performance. You have no audience to complain to as though life short-changed you. God has no time to create a misfit or a mediocrity. It is amazing how many people have lost their originality and relevance in trying to be what they are not purposed to be. Limitation is denying you your purpose. Every limitation in life is a product of imitation. To distort your purpose would be to significantly change who you are, because your purpose both informs and reveals your nature and your responsibilities. Everything you naturally have and inherently possess is necessary for you to fulfill your purpose. Your height, race, skin, color, language, physical features, and intellectual capacity are all designed by God for your purpose. Friends, you have no excuse not to get to the top.

When I discovered my purpose, life became amazingly swifter and sweeter. Doors started opening. More grace and favors started coming my way. I saw myself excelling at the same things many had been struggling to overcome. I saw the power of personal purpose in action. In fact, the book you are reading is visible evidence of this discovery. It is time to put meaning into your life as you discover your purpose.

# Chapter 9

## *Maximizing the Moment*

*So teach us to number our days, that we may apply our hearts unto wisdom.*

*Psalm 90:12*

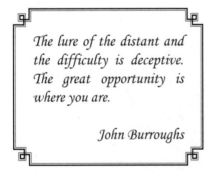

*The lure of the distant and the difficulty is deceptive. The great opportunity is where you are.*

*John Burroughs*

The moment you are in right now is a very important part of your life. Your future may depend on the sum total of actions you are taking right now. Your dreams, aspirations, and vision for life may depend on the number of hours you are spending or investing at the moment. We don't have all the time on earth to do what we want to do when we feel we want to do it. The word "now" best describes a productive dreamer. You already have been specially and divinely endowed with what you need to begin to create your future. Don't find yourself saying, "If only I had this . . . if only things were different . . . if only I had more money, then I could do what I am supposed to do." Never let what you think you can't do keep you from doing what you can do. Prolonged idleness paralyzes initiative because, to the hesitant mind, everything is impossible because it seems so.

## Why You Must Maximize the Moment

The moment you are in now is crucial and strategic in deciding your future. Yesterday is no longer within your control. Your failures, disappointments, sorrows, and successes of yesterday are but foregone issues. There is nothing you can do today to influence yesterday to become what it was not. Tomorrow is a dependent. It is just an open check, waiting for you to fill it out. No matter the amount of outcome you want, what you get in the future is just a result of what you saved today. If tomorrow is to bring success and greatness, then purpose, vision, dreams, focus, and hard work have to be sown today. Hence, today (the moment) is the most important part of your life. Life gives you not only what you desire but also what you deserve. What you deserve is a result of what you invest. Therefore, every man can be said to have what it takes to decide what he gets.

## The Moment Decides the Quality of Life

No person's life can be accurately measured by a number of days, for days lose their meaning when they stand in the face of eternity. The question isn't how *long* we live but how *well* we live. What matters are the moments we live life to the fullest.

Quality of life is not determined by material possessions. A man's success should be applauded but not worshipped. Real success consists of more than riches alone. You may have riches because of what you do, but wealth is what you are.

Everyone has the potential to have riches, because we are all endued with great wealth naturally. You are wealthy in opportunities, wealthy in creativity, and wealthy in the chance to prioritize your life, maximize your potential, and reassess your strengths. You are also wealthy because God loves you.

There is a mystery in the world of poverty. It is amazing that among the poor folks are men with unquantifiable strength, and also others who just lie around and let opportunities pass them by. The truth remains that it is not the level of engagements and activities in the moment that are important, but the worth of what you are actively engaged with in the moment.

In order to maximize your life, you have to minimize your load. You must decide what you will and will not take on. You must determine what is worthy of attention. Remember, not every situation that arises deserves your attention. You must direct your concentration to what's important. Some things should be dismissed as just nuisances.

You can deal with many things at the same time, but wisdom is needed in choosing which one to respond to and which one to ignore. This is the wisdom that will help you to maximize your life by maximizing the moment.

## Why You Must Start Now

Do not wait for special circumstances to act; use ordinary situations. Your day-to-day routine can become your vital port in beginning a journey that will take you to stardom. You don't need more strength, ability, or greater opportunity. Use what you have now. Everyone should row with the oars he has been given. You have your own oars of talents and gifts; why not launch out with them? True greatness consists of being great at little things. Don't grumble because you don't have what you want; be thankful you don't get what you deserve. A man named Walter Dwight put it this way: "'We must do something' is the unanimous refrain. 'You begin' is the deafening reply." Everyone believes something has to be done today for a better tomorrow. We sing it out in choruses, stanzas, and refrains, but we watch and wait indecisively on how to begin. I say, "Begin now."

You can never get much of anything done unless you go ahead and do it before everything is perfect. No one ever made a success of anything by first waiting until the conditions were just right. It's a waste of time to think about what you don't have; instead, spend your time on the task before you, knowing that the right performance of this hour's duties will be the best preparation for the years that follow it.

Personally, I have committed myself to a dream so big, but so comprehensive, that I work daily, maximizing the moment, investing my time and wealth of talents toward actualizing my dreams: building lives and restoring destinies across the world by the strong prophetic grace upon my life.

# Chapter 10

## *Thermometer or Thermostat*

*In all labor there is profit, but mere talk leads only to poverty.*

*Proverbs 14:23 (NASB)*

*Do all the good you can, in all the ways you can, and all the places you can, at all times you can, to all people you can, as long as you ever can.*

*John Wesley*

The prefix "thermo" means "heat." Life is like a hot furnace or an oven. Men are therefore likened to its regulatory and recording components, vis-à-vis the thermometer and the thermostat. These two components of an oven have the same operational base but do different things. The thermometer is used for measuring the change in temperature within the calibrated units. Fundamentally, the thermometer only measures what the thermostat regulates. The thermometer becomes the *talker*—always ready to convey to the furnace operator the extent of work the thermostat (the worker) has done

Some men are like the thermometer (talkers) while others, by virtue of choice and determination, have taken the form and duty of thermostats (workers), making the impacts for the thermometer to report. The thermometers are men with weird intentions. They like to cash their checks from a bank where they have no accounts. These are spectators in the football field of life—the self-appointed analysts. They dwell on the street called Volume-of-Words. Every conceivable idea is theirs, but none ever sees the land of reality. They have answers for every kind of question. These are the self-acclaimed communicators and news agents of the recent happenings in the city. No news, foreign or local, goes without their catch. These folks have every smart explanation for any kind of disappointing occurrence. They never get disappointed, because they never expect anything. They are charismatic, yet nothing tangible to boast of. They are charming, but harmful to associate with. They are busy with everything, but unable to grasp the real thing. You can start pinpointing men like this in your life. Men of this nature rarely get to the land of stars and achievers. Try to avoid them if you must move ahead.

## The Achiever's Mentality

On the other hand, thermostats are like men who understand that if you respond to life challenges the way they present themselves, they will remain a mountain before you, but if you treat those obstacles as what you want them to become, they will be transformed to what you want them to be. They believe that you draw nothing out of the bank of life except what you deposit in it. They understand that the difference between ordinary and extraordinary is that little extra. They are ocean-minded individuals who have discovered that every new ocean of possibility and greatness comes when you lose sight of the shore and move, by faith, down into the deep. As Helen Keller said, this group of persons understands that life is either a daring adventure or nothing. Giving excuses to them is tantamount to building a house of failures.

The thermostatic men are men of faith. These are men who have conquered doubts and the terror of fears. These rare characters believe, "Impossible is a word only found in the dictionary of fools [thermometers]" (Napoleon). The word "impossible" is never found on their lips, because they don't dwell in that realm. These men believe that what the mediocre call luck is where opportunity and preparation meet. "You can't consistently perform in a manner that is inconsistent with the way you see yourself" (Zig Ziglar).

These are men with defined personal pictures that are clear, vivid, and purposeful.

> *Doubt sees the obstacles; faith sees the way.*
> *Doubt sees the darkest night; faith sees the day.*
> *Doubt dreads to take a step; faith soars on high.*
> *Doubt questions, "Who believes"? "Faith," answers I.*
> —*Sam Amaga*

## The Choice Is Yours

From the aforementioned groups of people, the choice is left for you to make. Which category do you wish to belong to? Your answer to this question may not be as important as your reaction to it. Life holds so many potential opportunities for you that average life is no longer an acceptable life. John L. Mason describes mediocrities by saying, "They are the best of the worst and worst of the best." The ordinary life is a blow to the new creation. The Bible is emphatic in this.

"But ye are a chosen generation, a royal priesthood, an holy nation, a peculiar people [achievers, momentum makers, men of great impact]: That ye should shew forth [manifest, reveal, prove] the praise of him who hath called you out of darkness [poverty, foolishness, mediocrity, average life, ordinary life, failure, excuses, accusations, etc.] into his marvelous light [wisdom, ideas, creativity, relevance]" (1 Peter 2:9 KJV, emphasis mine).

Nothing can be more challenging than the above Bible verse. Imagine the purpose and expectations of God for your redeemed life. This is amazing! There is virtually no room for mediocrity in my own understanding of the new covenant believers. God has done more than is required to transform you from a thermometer into a thermostat. It is for you to regulate, organize, provoke, create, rebuild, and manifest the creativity, quality, and nature of God, your creator and father.

Recently, I met a friend whom I have known for a long time. He looked at me and said, "Godwin, I see all the great things that are happening in your life, and you are increasing in so many different ways. But as I began to look at your life, I became full of doubts as to what was happening in my life. It caused me to doubt myself, because I have not had the same success that you have."

I replied to him this way: "Friend, what happens in my life has nothing to do with what is happening in your life. The productive life is never an accident. Life gives you what you deserve and not just what you desire."

I feel most people fail because they work hard in measuring and comparing others with themselves, thereby limiting their potentials within the confines of other people's achievements. The Bible talks of people who measure themselves with others, thus showing that they lack wisdom.

Undue comparison saps the power of initiative.

# Chapter 11

## Your Purpose, Your Destiny

*Without counsel purposes are disappointed: but in the multitude of counselors they are established.*

Proverbs 15:22

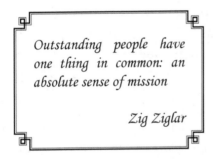

*Outstanding people have one thing in common: an absolute sense of mission*

Zig Ziglar

Having a purpose is more important than having talent in creating and shaping your life. There is presently an air of confusion surrounding teachings on success. The ordinary mind has found such teachings unworkable, and multitudes are being disappointed. But before you can begin thinking about becoming a success, you need to define what success is for you. You need to know it. Focus—right, focus—is the key to success.

Take the example of General George S. Patton of the US Army. Even as a young boy of barely seven, George had his purpose as clearly defined as the edge of a sword. It was pure and simple; he was to become a brigadier general. He was so committed to this that, like any model soldier, he stood at attention and saluted his father every morning.

As Patton grew through his teen years, he continued to do his daring best to achieve his purpose in life as only he could define it. He avidly read stories of the great military men of history. He even went further to study Persian, Greek, and Roman generals, battle formations, and medieval wars. His class reports featured themes of fame, glory, and heroism.

Patton was self-responsible to a fault. He learned early on that the prizes in life are earned through persistent efforts. It was sheer hard work that helped him overcome and graduate from West Point College. Likewise, through the course of his historic rise to fame, culminating in his promotion to full general of the US Army, he rode on no one's coattails. It was his honest, all-out effort directed by God that saw him to his end purpose every time.

As a plebe at West Point, he scribbled in his personal notebook the credo that would eventually help achieve his vision of becoming a general: "Do everything with all the snap and power you possess . . . when ordered to do a thing, carry out the spirit as well as the letter. Do all you can do, not only all you have to do."

Everyone who knew George Patton, or who has read about his life, has his own opinion of him. However, I believe all would agree that Patton was, above all, a man of purpose. He reached out and embraced history. In this sense, he fulfilled the destiny about which he often talked and wrote.

Regarding destiny, Patton said the following: "A man must know his destiny . . . if he does not recognize it, then he is lost. By this I mean, once, twice, or at the very most, three times, fate will reach out and tap a man on the shoulder . . . if he has the imagination, he will turn around and fate will point out to him what fork in the road he should take, if he has the guts, he will take it."

## Destiny Is a Kinetic Force

Having a purpose ordained of God is more important than having talents in creating and shaping your life.

Patton's example proves the above statement. You can "move mountains" with great resolve when you apply yourself persistently and consistently. That's why having a purpose, or a mission, is essential. Purpose, pursued, lands you in your destiny. Destiny is a kinetic force that pulls purpose to itself.

The questions remain: What are your goals? What do you aspire to be? What is your dream? Think of who you are today. Imagine yourself at your personal and professional best. Imagine feeling good about yourself in relation to your family and friends, neighbors, coworkers, ministry, and business associates. That is fulfillment! It is simply purpose defined and realized.

## Define Your Purpose

Purpose undefined is purpose confined. A confined purpose leads to frustrations and gross disappointments. Why do you think you are here on this earth? Your answer is your first step to being able to answer the question "What is your purpose?" A child can legitimately answer, "To be loved." An adult could best answer, "To love." Self-responsibility includes making choices about how to use your energies. Who will you help? Which course will you support and fight for? When you reach the point where you are full-time in your business, you'll more deeply understand what an American author once wrote "People say that what we're all seeking is a meaning for life. I don't think that's what we're really seeking. I think that what we're seeking is an experience of being alive, so that our life experiences on the purely physical plane will have resonances within our own innermost being and reality, so that we actually feel the rapture of being alive. That's what it's all finally about, and that's what these clues help us to find within ourselves."

Most of us want to feel what it means to be alive, but this is only possible when we are living a life guided by our self-defined purpose as ordained by God (rather than defined by other people). When we do so, we are likely to be better able to enjoy each passing day. Despite challenges, we will probably be more grateful for life and eager to make the most of it. Having a purpose helps self-responsible people be enthusiastic about life.

Do you believe a grim and stern demeanor is the sign of someone who is living self-responsibly? If your answer is yes, you may want to reconsider. Yes, there are gloomy people who are very responsible. However, these are generally people fulfilling responsibilities imposed on them by others (e.g., a boss or a commander). Living with a purpose is one of life's greatest joys. If you have the courage to search your soul, you will find your purpose. Many people live as if opportunity were death knocking on the door. Those who ignore opportunities and fail to define and work toward their purpose fall into a slow stagnation. Purpose naturally leads to prudent risk-taking, warding off stagnation and boredom.

When you take charge of your decisions and accept full responsibility for the outcomes, prudent risk-taking is easy. You can look for a direction to move in, which will help you recognize your purpose. As your purpose evolves, it will guide your investment of energies and resources into your business.

I was born into a family that was predominantly farmers, and I hated the rigors and burdens of subsistence farming. One morning, under drizzling showers of rain dripping down my body, with a small weeding hoe grasped loosely in my right hand and my mum shouting at me, I made a decision: that year was to be my last year as a little farm boy. I decided I must get a university degree to further beautify my purpose as a minister of the gospel—which was already manifesting in me at that early stage of my life—and thus maximize my potential for a life of fulfillment instead of struggling on the farm.

Your story can change for the better today if you believe God can do it for you.

# Chapter 12

## *March off the Map!*

*Brethren I count not myself to have apprehended. But this one thing I do forgetting those things which are behind and reaching forth unto things which are before, I press toward the mark for the price of the high calling of God in Christ Jesus.*

*Philippians 3:13–14*

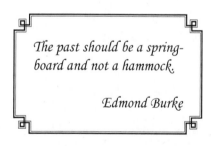

*The past should be a spring-board and not a hammock.*

*Edmond Burke*

One of the easiest diagnosable reasons for many failures in life is self-rejection due to past failures, sins, mistakes, and the inability to perform some tasks. These have become handy enemies to the present. The fruits of the present now stand at the mercy of the past.

The future becomes an unrealizable dream, and life begins to ebb away into a state of confusion and disillusion. Staying in the past is the greatest enemy of maximizing the privileges of today. Your life is no longer dependent on the past, because the past is irretrievable. Trying to call up the past is the easiest way to lose grip of the present and allow the future to further run ahead of you. It is of little wonder why the devil has found an easy armamentarium via the power of false guilt and rejection as a result of past events. This stands against the will and purpose of God. However, it is only a clear understanding of the diabolic antics of the devil, and entrusting your life to God for healing, that will liberate you from every damage of the past and rescue you from that guilt and rejection. "Some people stay so far in the past that the future is gone before they get there" (John Mason).

Life is designed to function one moment at a time. Time is the most obedient instrument of God designed to guide us on earth toward fulfilling our divine purposes. Every event in life is so timed that adequate attention should be paid to our daily activities. Doing the best thing at the wrong time could mean putting a round peg into a square hole. Because we are living in a timed world, every past event in our life should be counted as a foregone alternative that ushered in the present. The present is our only manageable opportunity to create our desired future. In other words, the productive life is never an accident; rather, it is the resultant effect of a proper management of the past, maximization of the present, and manifestation of the future through positive approaches to attitudes and confessions.

## Learn to Forgive yourself and Forget the Past

"Remember ye not the former things neither consider the things of old. Behold, I will do a new thing: now it shall spring forth: shall ye not know it? I will even make a way in the wilderness, and rivers in the desert" (Isaiah 43:18–19).

As I searched through Scriptures, I discovered that our God is a God of new things. He is always doing new things; He has no time left to call up the past. I feel God understands how toxic it is to cloud the present with the failures of the past. The Bible has been described as a prophetic book. And I wonder what, actually, is prophecy? It is speaking into the future—is that not so? Now, if the book containing all the foundation blocks of any known real success is described as a book that speaks about the future, how swiftly our success will emerge and how glorious it will be if we shall learn to forget those things that are behind (failures, sins, guilt, rejections, hurts, etc.) and reach forth unto those things that are before us (dreams, visions, purpose, glorious destiny, etc.).

To see what is behind you, you must face and walk backward. No one faces the sun and yet beholds his shadow behind him. You are either focused on the sun and move forward or you are bothered about your distorted shadow (image) and retrogress. Sin, guilt, and rejection are inevitable with every man, but God has made a way of escape from such cankerworms. Every confessed sin is a forgiven sin and should be a forgotten sin. God is ever willing to forgive us if we are willing to admit and confess our sins. But before every man lies a world of opportunities and personalities packaged with untapped potentials. It would be a gross failure to live without knowing when we outlived our relevance as a result of wasted years and the propensity to dwell in the past.

From the autobiography of Dr. Benjamin Carson, I would like to recount the wonderful story of a small, ghetto-dwelling black boy in Detroit, Michigan, USA. His past was nothing to write home about. At the age of eight, his father left home to return no more, so he grew up without fatherly care, direction, shelter, or love. Not too long after that, his visibly overburdened mother developed psychological problems that almost caused her to become a psychiatric case. So the young boy, Ben, and his elder brother, Curtis, were both left to the mercy of family friends.

To Ben, getting to college seemed to be impossible in the presence of severe hardship coupled with the absence of both parents. Thus, a life of struggle, rejection, depression, repression, guilt, sorrow, and failure greeted the young Ben. His mentality was obviously retarded as a result of the traumatic experiences of his childhood. But all of these things would be momentary. No sooner had Ben realized that life waits for nobody nor sympathizes with anybody than he launched out to find the reason for his existence. He marched off the map! He tore through those self-limiting obstacles that were haunting him. He pressed on toward the mark for the prize of the high calling of God over his life in Christ Jesus.

## Here Is the Price and the Prize

"In 1987, Dr. Ben Carson gained worldwide recognition for his part in the first separation of Siamese twins joined at the back of the head. Carson pioneered again in a rare procedure known as hemispherectomy, giving children without hope a second chance at life through a daring operation in which he literally removes one half of their brain.

"Such breakthroughs aren't unusual for Ben Carson. He's been beating the odds since he was a child. Raised in inner-city Detroit by a mother with a third-grade education, Ben lacked motivation. He had terrible grades. And a pathological temper threatened to put him in jail.

"But Sonya Carson convinced her son that he could make something of his life even though everything around him said otherwise. Trust in God, a relentless belief in his own capabilities, and sheer determination catapulted Ben from failing grades . . . to the top of his class—and beyond to a Yale scholarship . . . the University of Michigan medical school . . . and finally, at age thirty-three, the directorship of pediatric neurosurgery at John Hopkins Hospital in Baltimore, Maryland. Today Dr. Ben Carson holds twenty honorary doctorates and is the possessor of a long string of honors and awards."

That was the failure, the ghetto boy, little Ben, who now is Professor Ben Carson with innumerable degrees and awards. Dr. Carson was never as privileged as some of you reading this book. He deliberately refused to cave in to the ignoble demands of his childhood predicaments. I believe I am speaking to some little Bens in the ghetto side of their lives now. The choice is left for you to make: become a ghetto master or another Professor Ben Carson, with strings of degrees, honors, and awards. Friends, it is time to march off the map. Put meaning into your life.

# Chapter 13

## *Destined to Deliver*

*For I can do everything with help of Christ who gives
me the strength I need.*

*Philippians 4:13 (NLT)*

> *Grow where you are planted,
> begin to weave, and God
> will give the thread.*
>
> *German proverb*

You already have been given what you need to begin to create and deliver your future. Don't find yourself saying, "If only I had this . . . if only things were different . . . if only I had more, then I could do what I am supposed to do." People always overstate the importance of things they don't have.

Never let what you think you can't do keep you from doing what you can do. Prolonged idleness paralyzes initiative because, to the hesitant mind, everything is impossible because it seems so. Don't wait for special circumstances to act; use ordinary situations. We don't need more strength, ability, or greater opportunity. Use what you have. Everyone must row with the oars he has been given. As John Burroughs said, "The lure of the distant and its difficulty is deceptive. The great opportunity is where you are."

What you can do now is the only influence you have over your future. No one can be happy until he has learned to enjoy what he has rather than worry over what he doesn't have.

It's a waste of time to think about what you don't have. Instead, spend your time on the task before you, knowing that the right performance of this hour's duties will be the best preparation for the years that follow it. If you wish to arrive at your desired tomorrow, you must not continue to look backward. The more you look backward, the less you'll see forward. The only time looking backward is allowed is to recall a testimony that will boost your efforts toward your present calling.

Count not on the losses of yesterday; rather dwell on the blessings of today (read Philippians 4:6). Yesterday ended last night, so you have only today. It is more valuable to look ahead and prepare than to look back and regret. Don't let regrets replace your dreams. As John Barrymore said, "A man is not lost until regrets take the place of dreams."

Regret looks back. Worry looks around. Vision looks up. Life can be understood backward, but it must be lived forward. If history were all that mattered, librarians would be the only successful people in the world. The past should only be viewed with gratitude for the good things. The events of the past are the star of your fresh start. Consider this: When David agreed to take on Goliath, everyone else thought he would lose; in fact, they were sure of it! But as a young lad, David had killed a lion and a bear and had not been afraid. David recalled with faith and assurance the testimonies of his past. The past became the springboard upon which he launched his faith. He was confident that he had to deliver. He had delivered before by the same almighty power of Jehovah. He said to Goliath, "You come to me with a sword, a spear and a Javelin, but I come to you in the name of the Lord of host" (1 Samuel 17:45 AB).

Before you can take delivery of your future, you must allow the Lord to fight the present battles for you. No tension! You must be still (have confidence with faith) and see the salvation of the Lord (see Exodus 14:13). If there are giants in your life today, you can always trust God, who causes us to triumph (see 2 Corinthians 2:14). Tap into the blessings and make your way prosperous by speaking Word-based confessions over your life daily.

Say what it is you want to see, and begin the climb upward. If you're not saying anything, you're not creating anything. Words are the raw materials used in creating your demands in the spiritual realm.

You were created to shine like a star in the universe (see Daniel 12:3). Your life should reflect the goodness of God and point to Him. You have a mission that is uniquely yours to carry out on His behalf. I can't do what God called you to do, because I've got my own mission too.

Decide in your heart to stop doing things the world's way. Set the example. Be a trendsetter; don't follow the trend! Renew your mind with the Word of God and lay hold of the blessings that give you the edge over the world and cause you to rise above your circumstances (see Romans 12:2). Whatever God has to say about it is what you must believe and confess.

Child of God, let Him be Lord in your life today by submitting to His will. He knows what lies ahead, and He knows how to get you from where you are to where you should be. If you walk in obedience to His will, you can't lose. You are a perfect winner!

# Chapter 14

## *Creator or Critic*

*Let us not therefore Judge one another any more; but judge this rather, that no man put a stumbling block or an occasion to fall in his brother's way.*

*Romans 14:13*

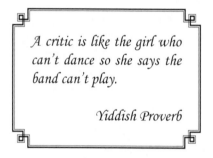

*A critic is like the girl who can't dance so she says the band can't play.*

*Yiddish Proverb*

Momentum-makers all share one trait—they attract criticism. How you respond to that criticism will determine the rate of your momentum's impact. There has never been any powerful minister of God who has operated without thunderous criticism trailing behind him. It appears that the more the impact one has, the more criticism one generates. There are no exceptions. Great gospel generals like Billy Graham, Smith Wigglesworth, Oral Roberts, Katherine Kulman, Benson Idahosa, and David Oyedepo, to name but a few, have faced great, damaging criticisms.

All great people receive great criticism. Learn to accept and expect the unjust criticism for your great goals and accomplishments. Your act of maturity as a momentum-maker and a creator is measured by not only what you make happen but also how you handle what happens to you, including criticism.

It can be beneficial to receive constructive criticism from those who have your best interests at heart, but you're not obligated to respond to those who contribute nothing to your pursuit. Don't ever give time to a critic; instead, invest it with a friend. Look at how a man called Edward Gibbon puts it: "I never make the mistake of arguing with people for whose opinion I have no respect."

You must not spend your time with someone who does not respect what God has called you to do. The critic is the wrong person to convince. As long as you are on your assignment, let rain and brimstone fall; stick to your vision. Note this: The devil is interested in your assignment; he will use distractions through the weapon of criticism to dislodge you and destroy your vision. But you can choose to allow him or not.

It's a thousand times easier to criticize than to create. That's why critics are never problem-solvers. As Dale Carnegie put it, "Any fool can criticize, condemn, and complain, and most do." My feeling is that the person who says it cannot be done should not interrupt the one who is doing it. Just remember, when you are kicked from behind, it means you are out in front. You see, backbiters always stay at the back, biting. The critic never stays in front; otherwise, he won't see what to criticize. Because critics comment on everything as spectators, they cheer and jeer all day and go home without any award or prize. Critics know not the answer, having not probed deep enough to know the questions. Richard Le Gallienne once stated, "A critic is a man created to praise greater men than himself, but he is never able to find them."

I once told a friend that the reason I am unruffled by criticism is that I need both my friends and foes (critics) to boost the strength of my fans. The critic is convinced that the chief purpose of sunshine is to cast shadows. He doesn't believe anything, but he still wants you to believe him. Like a cynic, he always knows the "price of everything and the value of nothing" (Oscar Wilde).

Don't waste time responding to your critics if you must remain in the hall of fame, because you owe nothing to a critic.

The critics spend their whole time searching for what's right, but then they can't seem to find time to practice it. Remember, knowing what is right and then not doing it is wrong. Your life story is written not with a pen, but with your actions. To do nothing is the way to be nothing. Be big; don't become a critic. As Julia Seton put it, "We have no more right to put our discordant states of mind into lives of those around us and rub them of their sunshine and brightness than we have to enter their houses and steal their silverware."

Remember that in criticizing others, you will work overtime for no pay. Don't spend the little productive time you have as a thermometer, reading and recording other people's actions, rather than becoming a thermostat; start off with an action!

A colleague in an institution I worked at some time ago was the self-imposing, intimidating, and overly possessive type. Everyone appeared very small in her judgment, compared to her. She practically dominated everybody around her, but I, having dealt with many personalities of her type, drafted a plan of action to adequately humble her. I practically upgraded myself to have an edge over her on the job. She struggled to catch up, but failed woefully. When she discovered that I had been continually creating waves among our colleagues and beyond, and that my popularity had soared very high, she turned into a critic. I became' a thorn in her flesh.

The more I tried to get close and dislodge that ugly spirit of criticism and competition from her, the more she despised me. As every critic would have it, her ignominious character betrayed her into the hands of a person who had the right to expel her from service. The incident humbled her so much that it took her a month to gather herself together again. Today, she is back to normal. Never throw mud. If you do, you may hit your mark, but you will have dirty hands. Don't be a cloud because you failed to become a star. Instead, "give so much time to the improvements of yourself that you have no time to criticize others" (Christian D. Larson). Spend your time and energy creating, not criticizing.

*A good thing to remember.*
*A better thing to do.*
*Work with the constructing gang.*
*Not the wrecking crew.*

# Chapter 15

## *Define and Establish Your Purpose*

*Without counsel purpose are disappointed; but in the multitude of counselors they are established.*

*Proverbs 15:22*

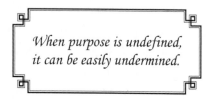

*When purpose is undefined, it can be easily undermined.*

Purpose gives meaning and value to our lives. It provides us with a reason to become the person we are meant to be. Most importantly it offers us the opportunity to contribute to others. It is well known that those who retire from their professions without future plans or direction often have shorter life spans than those who do make plans. Purpose establishes in your own heart and mind that others need you and your talents. Countless studies have demonstrated the negative impact depression and a lack of self-esteem have on physical health. Establishing a purpose can assist you in maintaining a healthier lifestyle.

Always conclude within yourself that you have something more to offer. You may have to communicate to others that you have a certain ability or talent. Then pursue the opportunities available to you that will allow you to give what you would enjoy giving the most. For example, if you love spending time with children, build your business so you can get free of your job; you will then have the time to volunteer at a local children's hospital or Sunday school, or operate a child-care center.

Purpose enables you to enjoy more of life's pleasures. It's the greatest when your purpose becomes your pleasure. For example, if my purpose is to motivate others to achieve success, then no other career is going to give me as much satisfaction as doing that. Therefore, it is not practical for me to spend a great deal of time fixing automobile engines. It's not where my talents lie, it's not what I have defined as my purpose, it's not what would give me optimal pleasure, and it's not what enables me to serve to my greatest ability and make a difference.

## How to Define Your Purpose

It is important to both you and others to discover and honestly acknowledge what your main purpose in life really is, or what you would like it to be. There are six questions that can assist you in defining your purpose. You can also discover whether your work and outside activities are helping you fulfill your purpose.

1. What purpose is provided by your job?
2. What purpose do you expect yourself to fulfill through your business (e.g., represent the highest standard of the business to the public, maintain a teamwork attitude, or promote the business mission by helping others succeed so you can make your dreams come true)?
   a. What personal attributes will shape my purpose?
   b. What do I do well? What skills do I possess that clearly reflect my talents?
   c. What would I love to do? What would I do if time and money were not issues?
   d. What do others appreciate about me?

    e. What areas am I weak in? Are any of these skills necessary for accomplishing what I would love to do?

    f. What do others not appreciate about me? What do I need to change to accomplish what I would love to do?

    g. What is my attitude like? Do people want to be around me?

3. What do you want out of life? What does it mean for you to be alive? What are you actually living to fulfill?

4. What activities are you involved in outside of your job that allow you to use your talent to do what you love to do?

5. If you have discovered that neither your job activities nor those outside work help you to fulfill your purpose, what can you do to accelerate building your business to move in this direction?

6. What steps are you going to take (e.g., counsel with your mentors or someone qualified to speak into your life)?

By answering these questions, you'll be better equipped to determine the fundamentals for your purpose in life. What do you think it is? If you feel you don't know, use your imagination, think, and, above all, ask God. "If you want to know the purpose of a product, ask the manufacturer" (Myles Monroe).

No one can effectively define you purpose for you. Your creator who designed you still retains your operation manual. God has not delivered such a manual to another person. Truly, by virtue of keen observation, someone can define your purpose, but it will never be accurate. The fact is that you live your purpose daily, but until you are willing to discover, define, and establish it, it will remain absurd to you. Confusion sets in when purpose is undefined. Waste and abuse are usually the resultant effects of undefined purpose.

When purpose is discovered, it must be boldly penned down and meditated upon. (For example, the purpose of one of my friends is to build business networking that spans the globe, to generate funds necessary to support a home for homeless children.) When you write your purpose down on paper, remember what John Wesley once said: "Make all you can. Invest all you can, give all you can."

## Praise God! You've Done It!

Good for you! Let yourself come away from this chapter feeling exuberant. Yes, the possibilities you once imagined are now becoming real. The key to your success is defining your own purpose, which you've just had an opportunity to do (see Daniel 1:8). Your personal action plan is beginning to unfold.

With the strength of self-responsibility as your support, and a well-defined purpose as your guide, your preparations for embarking on the staircase of success are two-thirds complete. Bon voyage!

# Chapter 16

## Elevate Your Attitude and Enthusiasm

*And the keeper of the prison committed to Joseph's hand all the prisoners' that were in the prison, and whatsoever they did there, he was the doer of it . . . because the Lord was with him, and that which he did, the Lord made it to prosper.*

Genesis 39:22–23

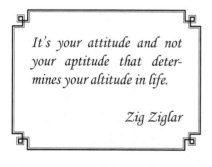

*It's your attitude and not your aptitude that determines your altitude in life.*

*Zig Ziglar*

William James once said, "It is one's attitude at the beginning of a difficult undertaking which, more than anything else, will determine its successful outcome." In fact, you can alter your life and affect the lives of those around you simply by changing your attitude. Prepare yourself to develop and maintain an elevated attitude and enthusiasm, and give your life a jolt!

"Attitude" is defined as a state of mind expressing a certain opinion, while "enthusiasm" is defined as a strong excitement of feeling; something inspiring, zeal, terror, warmth, or eagerness. Elevating your attitude and enthusiasm is an express step on the staircase of success. Think about it. How you express yourself helps to determine the ideas and feelings people have about you. It also influences how fast you move toward your dreams.

Learn how to express rather than impress! Be enthusiastically sincere, especially in building your business. It attracts people like a magnet! Take a look at the prison life of Joseph as found in Genesis 39 and 40. He was wrongly accused and incarcerated in the prison. But by elevating his attitude and enthusiasm, the prison warden thought within himself, *Joseph must be a sincere, strange, and innocent fellow.* Because of Joseph's attitude and enthusiasm, he magnetically attracted many of the prisoners to himself; he endeared himself to everyone. He instantly became their chief spokesman and leader. When the warden observed this, he deliberately handed over the prison activities into the hands of Joseph—a prisoner. It is amazing! But the truth is that Joseph could command the respect and obedience of all other prisoners; the prison warder lacked this ability. The Bible further says, "Whatever he did, the Lord prospered it."

When you learn to honor and respect yourself more and you appreciate the possibilities that exist for you, guess what happens? A natural tendency to shine kicks in; you find yourself on your way to becoming a leader. An elevated attitude and enthusiasm are marks of a leader, and esprit de corps (enthusiastic comradeship) is the mark of a group led by that person.

An elevated attitude begins when you have a dream and start to resolve the conflicts in your life. In our hectic society, many people are often fragmented and unfocused in their thoughts and behaviors. They may be in survival mode, not looking at the bigger picture of what they really want. An elevated attitude helps you have the desire and energy to remain focused on what you want to accomplish.

Your elevated attitude and enthusiasm are keys to inspiring others to also take actions in their lives and callings. When you are self-responsible, define your life's purpose, and stop making excuses (i.e., don't blame anybody or anything), your life will be different. As you forgive and direct the energy previously wasted on resentment and anger to where you know it can make a difference, you'll feel better about yourself. You will likely want to share this revelation with others. And that's where your attitude and enthusiasm come in.

When you wake up in the morning, are you happy? Do you say, "Good God, it's morning!" or "Good morning, God"? Do you look at your spouse next to you in bed and say, "I love you"? Does he or she smile about that? Is your glass half-empty or half-full? Your attitude is one of the first indicators that tell others what kind of person you are. As Dr. Robert Schuler says, "Happy is the person who is motivated to be a beautiful human being."

Be positive with other people, and be positive with yourself. Some of your self-talk may be negative. If so, you need to change that. Talk positively to yourself and expect to be more successful. If you aren't careful, challenges can dump you into the trap of negativity and discouragement. Circumstances can affect your attitude only if you let them. Get out from "under the circumstances." Face your challenges with an attitude of "this, too, shall pass"; you'll find it a lot easier than facing them with a negative attitude.

## How to Measure Your Attitude

You can measure your attitude by the way other people react to you. When you're positive, people are more likely to respond positively to you. If you're negative, and a real headache to be around, forget it. Other people are likely to react the same way and avoid you when possible. Most people don't want to be around negativity. They have enough of their own challenges. They need to be uplifted rather than more depressed. Of course, you may attract other negative people to join you in the muck and mire of your attitude. They will only contribute to your negativity and lack of success. It's like spiraling downward.

The more you know yourself, the better you can understand and work on your own unskillful behavior. The more you accept yourself and other people, the more positive you'll be. When you look at life as an opportunity rather than a burden, a struggle, or a headache, you'll have a more positive attitude and greater enthusiasm. This takes time and energy, but it's worth it if you must fly high.

Whenever possible, associate with people with positive attitudes and stay enthusiastic. Do you know that attitude and enthusiasm follow the laws of physics? One of Newton's laws states that an object at rest tends to remain at rest unless acted upon by another force. Also, an object in motion tends to remain in motion unless acted upon by another force. This is also true for people's attitudes, which will stay negative unless influenced by a positive attitude. Attitude and enthusiasm can be the force you need to get beyond negativity and to the outcomes you want.

# Chapter 17

## *Shoot for Stardom*

*And of the children of Issacher, which were men that had understanding of the times, to know what Israel ought to do: The heads of them were two hundred, and their brethren were at their commandment.*

1 Chronicles 12:32

> It is the depth of your understanding that determines the height of your outstanding results.

Quick understanding is one of your new creation privileges. For any change to take place in your life, you need a charged mind that guarantees surpassing understanding. Every destiny is designed in the mold of mentality. When a man's mentality is reconstructed, there is always a concurrent increase in productivity. Obviously, we need miracles above our necks, especially in this dispensation.

Becoming a star is a debt you owe to your re-created personality. It cost God Jesus to give you the re-created mind you have now. You can't afford to disappoint Him. By virtue of your new status, whatever is affordable by God has been made available to you. You are born again, and born into a world of limitless opportunities. Everything is waiting for your choice. The earlier you make the choice, the better.

To be ordinary is a blow to your new status in Christ. You have to consciously refuse to be down, because there is a place for you at the top. Employing your quickened understanding positions you strategically in the plan of God. Truly, understanding this new perspective will set you on a new pedestal. At a time when the whole of Israel was in a dilemma as to whom to follow as their king, confusion and frustration, coupled with anarchy, were the order of the day, but among the twelve tribes of Israel was the "insignificant" tribe of Issacher. Prior to now, nothing was known of them either in the priesthood or kingship. However, Scriptures emphasize that they were men of great and usual understanding.

Their understanding of the times ("time" here means, "event," "period," or "season") placed the entire Israel under their command. They knew it was time for King David to be crowned. Because of their in-depth understanding, two hundred of them became highly respected military commanders and leaders.

Your size, color, race, or education cannot limit your vision and achievement in life as much as your lack of understanding can. Irrespective of your geographical location, you can launch yourself into stardom by acquiring a refined mentality.

Men who die in the valley are men who fail to place value on whom they are; they do not die simply because they find themselves in the valley of life.

Because you carry the force of creation, you cannot afford to die in frustration. It is lack of purpose in life that breeds confusion, and when confusion goes unchecked, frustration is the result. Never be deceived that it is all over with you. As long as you keep on aspiring, you will never expire. It is when you refuse to aspire that you start expiring. Old age is a thing of the mind. You may have retired, but you can refuse to be tired. The quickest way to enter the grave is to put your hands up and give up. As long as you keep on working, you can't be sick, because you can't be sick and be working. Your sense is superior to your strength. If you must get up there, you have to engage your mind. Nothing is as creative as the mind you are carrying now. You have been struggling all alone on your own way to the top to no avail. I prescribe to you one thing: engage your mind now! By strength shall no one prevail (see 1 Samuel 2:8).

Every notable impact and every breakthrough contained in the *Guinness Book of World Records* is purely a product of the mind. There is always a sitting down (time of reasoning) before any standing up.

Now look at this: *"And they said, go to let us build us a city and a tower, whose top may reach unto heaven; and let us make us a name, lest we be scattered abroad upon the face of the whole earth. And the Lord came down to see the city and the tower, which the children of men builded. And the Lord said, Behold the people is one, and they have all one language. And this they begin to do; and now nothing will be restrained from them, which they have imagined to do"* (Genesis 11:4–6). This is amazing! The first time men sat down and engaged their minds to work, divinity was threatened. The Trinity became uneasy. A state of emergency was declared on planet earth. No angel could stop these men from accomplishing their plan. God had to personally come down to arrest the situation.

Simply put, humanity is still an amazing creation. I wish your eyes were open to comprehend the magnitude of the creative powers you possess! When you understand this truth, you are on your way to the top. The fall of man was the evidence that the devil was scared of the power God had bestowed on man. The devil, in his wildest imagination and furthest projection, could not understand why God would have given me and you the same mind and spirit in Him. The devil understood that if nothing were done quickly, perpetual damnation would befall him; hence his subtle intervention and, subsequently, the fall of man.

Notwithstanding, the same mind and spirit have been restored back to us via the sacrifice of Jesus. This time around we possess not only the mind and spirit, but also the same nature of God (see John 1:4). We are doubly more dangerous than the men of the tower of Babel. It is obvious why the devil has denied this revelation from the church for a long time. The church also has taken the reactive side instead of a proactive stance. By suppressing men's mentally, the devil has succeeded in deceiving the church to accept poverty, sickness, sorrow, and failure as part of the sacrifice we must pay to enter the kingdom of God, as if the sacrifice of Jesus needed amendments. Nothing can be further from the truth (see 3 John 3)!

Praise God! There is now a knowledge explosion. You can be a slave to those lies as long as you want to, but I charge you, friend—listen! You are too loaded to fail. You are too privileged to go down. You are too important to be disregarded. Your opinion must count. You must not allow a vacuum in your life. The top is your place, and you'll not want to miss your position. It is time for the church to teach the world. It is time for us to liberate the world. You can be a liberator instead of a liability. Your mind must be set to work if you are to get to the top.

# Chapter 18

## Change Is the Challenge of Growth

*If a man die, shall he live again? All the days of my appointed time will I wait, till my CHANGE COME.*

Job 14:14

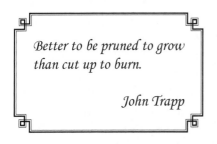

*Better to be pruned to grow than cut up to burn.*

John Trapp

Change is an inevitable factor on your journey to the top. How you manage change determines what you will reap out of it. Every change happening to you is like a two-edged sword. You can choose which side to make use of. You can never make maximum impact until you have a mastery of change management.

Moreover, every breakthrough in life is the product of a breakout (change) from status quo ante. And every change is traceable to a charge. You must constantly change your sails if you are to stay on course.

The late American astronaut James Irwin said, "You might think going to the moon was most scientific project ever, but they literally 'threw us' in the direction of the moon. We had to adjust our course every ten minutes and landed only inside fifty feet of the five-hundred-mile radius of our target." Now imagine what would have happened without the constant adjustments that Irwin and his colleagues were laboriously engaged in every ten minutes of the journey. On that mission, every change, no matter how small, was essential to their success. On your journey to the top, constant changes are inevitable. Without those changes, you will deliberately miss your target. It is the challenge of those changes that ushers you into a new realm of operation. No man ever gets to the top by accident. The fact is that the road to success is always under construction; no one has a mastery of it yet. Get ready for a change that will lift you to the top!

"When you can't change the direction of the wind, adjust your sails" (H. Jackson Brown Jr.). We cannot become what we need to be by remaining what we are. People hate change, yet it is the only thing that brings growth. There is nothing so permanent as change. Whatever the case, keep on adjusting your sail until you get to the top. You cannot afford to be tossed up and down uncontrollably, like a boat in the midst of a terrific tempest. The change must come with its terrible challenges, but get ready to celebrate your breakthrough afterward. However, all depends on how you manage the change. You can either submit helplessly to the demands of negative change or harness the situation and turn it around for greater productivity.

Your refusal to accept the present is a direct invitation for a change. It is wise to call for a change, because it takes wisdom to change your mind. Fools never do such things. They are stuck once and for all, even when they are draining down to the dregs of life. Some stay in the same job month after month, year after year, with no improvement, no growth, and no freedom, only to end up with a wooden sculpture called a long service award. Well, what is the value of a long service award compared to your wasted, unproductive lifetime? People should get smarter these days. You cannot be rich in any job. You must learn how to create things for yourself with the mind God gave you. To be conceited in your heart is to be a fool. It is a sign of strength to make changes when necessary. It is true that everybody favors progress but only a few pray for change. Most people are willing to change not because they see the light, but because they feel the heat. But you need the light for direction, not the heat.

Some people are still where they are today not because they enjoy it but simply because they are afraid of change. You've lost every passion for that job; there is no possibility of promotion, no satisfaction or fulfillment, and no future or fortune, yet you are stuck to it as though a spell has been cast upon you. You can never maximize your lifetime if you are forever attached to your comfort zone. Your comfort zone is the worst place to stay. It gives the impression that all is well, but in reality your visions and aspirations are being wasted. Consequently, you will begin to expire.

Nothing is made to be static. Great opportunities are not found in your comfort zone. They are located right inside the challenges of change. Men are still making great impacts in every field of life. The world has never seen the end to the discoveries and inventions in information and communications technology (ICT), business, transportation, power, and even the ministry. Men with great and amazing ideas are yet to be born. Those living have ideas yet to be manifested. You, too, can be one of them! Everything is changing; that is why you must be moving—constantly in motion. Current great ideas still need changes, adaptations, and modifications in order to prosper and succeed. Henry Ford forgot to put a reverse gear in his first automobile (funny—that car would get you there but might not come back!). Few knew of his oversight. Because he changed, few didn't know of his success. Success and growth are unlikely if you always do things the way you've always done them. When you stop changing, you stop growing.

I have a strong thirst for change. In fact, change has become my second nature. I find it difficult staying stagnant and doing the same thing over and over again no matter how comfortable that zone is. Something in me often makes me uncomfortable with unnecessary repetitions. Someone observed me for some time and dubbed me a transformer. I think that clearly explains my nature. I have a conviction that whatever is good can be made better, the better changed to the best, and the best transformed to excellence. I live by this conviction.

I charge you today: commit yourself to excellence from the start. No legacy is so rich as excellence. The quality of your life will be in direct proportion to your commitment to excellence, regardless of what you choose to do. Excellence is a product of change. Nothing gets better until the good is worked on by someone. Gold remains ordinary and crude unless someone uses a furnace to refine it. You, too, can gain control of that circumstance in your life. Transform it to your desires and reap excellence as your reward.

# Chapter 19

## The Sky Is Not Your Limit

*Now unto Him that is able to do exceeding abundantly above all that we ask or think according to the power that worketh in us.*

*Ephesians 3:20*

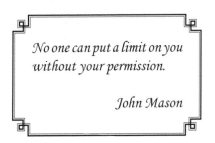

*No one can put a limit on you without your permission.*

*John Mason*

Every man's limit is a function of the extent of his dream. No one has ever reached the top by chance. No amount of accidental success can bring you to your dreams in life. Every success is a true manifestation of a commitment to a purpose. Purpose is the mother of all destinies, the master of motivations, and the preserver of dreams. Every breakthrough in life came as a result of constant impacts made toward one's dream. There is no accidental success because it ends accidentally.

You have been told the sky is your limit. But that is only true for as long as you keep the sky above you and give it the monstrous status of an impenetrable wrought-iron lid over you. Until you begin to knock off every self-imposed limit, you will never be able to break through the normal environmental obstacles that preclude every major success.

Through this book, you have received the delivery of keys that will open those doors of your life with the inscription "OUT OF BOUNDS." Truly, boundaries are for men who are bound and chained by their shallow level of dreams. But if you must escape the ordinary to be counted among the extraordinary, the hour has come for you to rise up and break every bind limiting you.

As you embark on these unusual adventures into the world of the extraordinary, expect colleagues and friends to stand aloof and yell at you. Some will laugh and scorn you. Others will prescribe the psychiatrist for you, just as Jesus's detractors said to Him, "He is beside Himself," "He has gone out of His senses," "He is possessed by Beelzebub, the prince of demons," etc. Always bear in mind that both friends and foes make up your fans. The world presses against a man who is confused and does not know where he is going, but steps aside to the man who knows where he is going. They will laugh at you, but you will laugh last. Look at the following great minds and inventors and what happened to them as they marched off the map toward prominence:

- **Eli Whitney** was laughed at when he showed his cotton gin. His friends wondered whether he had gone crazy. "How can you separate cotton from the seed with this shabby metal structure you joined together?" they probably asked in doubt. But today he is a celebrated inventor.

- **Thomas Edison** had to install his electric light free of charge in an office building before anyone would even look at it. In fact, he was even cautioned not to showcase his invention, as people feared he might burn down their houses. Yet Thomas Edison has contributed to life more than any scientist I know. Check it out! Tell me what life would have looked like without electricity. It proves the statement that every major breakthrough is the resultant effect of a major breakaway from numerous obstacles. Your life will remain a miracle until you remove the limit from yourself. Until your determination to die empty becomes your obsession, you may never live beyond where you are now. I pray this simple commitment prayer daily: "Father, I want to leave this earth empty. I don't want to return any talent you gave me unutilized. I don't want the graveyard to inherit any talent I should have used to better my world. Lord, cause me to leave this world a man exhausted of all potential. In Jesus's name. Amen." I pray that this be your daily prayer as well.

Beware of those who stand aloof and greet each venture with reproof. The world would stop if things were run by men who said, "It can't be done." Most such men are easily found among our friends and colleagues. They act out of either envy or jealousy. But remember, if you must dance to the tune of your friends' music, then you are sure to be frustrated. You must dictate which music you want, and that will determine which steps of the dance you will use in order to make a wonderful concert.

"Seek and ye shall find" (Matthew 7:7). We attain only in proportion to what we attempt. More people are persuaded into believing in nothing than believing too much. Jesus said, "According to your faith [dream, expectation] be it unto you" (Matthew 9:29). You are never as far from the answer as it appears. It's never safe or accurate to look into the future without faith. The picture you have about Jesus determines the future you expect from Him. If He is merely a good man with good ideas—a world leader of His time—then I know you are a historian expecting a historian's reward (e.g., dwelling in the past). But if to you believe Christ is the son of God; our advocate before God; the King of Kings and Lord of Lords; the master who holds all powers, including success, in His hands, then I know you are on your way to the inexhaustible riches exclusively found in Christ.

A lot of people no longer hope for the best; they just hope to avoid the worst.

Many of us have heard opportunity knocking at our door, but by the time we unhooked the chain, pushed back the handle, turned two locks, and shut off the burglar alarm—it was gone! Too many people spend their lives looking around or looking behind when God says to look up. The sky is not the limit!

Always bear in the mind that not all obstacles are bad. In fact, an opportunity's favorite disguise is an obstacle. Conflict is simply an obstacle on the road to your miracle. Such a fight is good; it is proof that you haven't quit. Any day you stop daring, you will start dying. At any time you stop taking chances, you will stop making advances. You definitely need risks to rise. No man has ever reached the sky without scars.

Growth and success don't eliminate obstacles. They create new ones. Thomas Castle said, "The block of granite which was an obstacle in the pathway of the weak becomes a stepping-stone in the pathway of the strong." Obstacles provide an opportunity to grow, not die. Even in the midst of trials, God wants growth and promotion for you. Obstacles can temporarily detour you, but only you can make you stop. The devil can temporarily detour you, but only you can permanently stop you. Obstacles reveal what we truly believe and who we really are. They introduce you to yourself. Your struggle may be lasting, but it is not everlasting.

# Chapter 20

## You Can Make a Difference

*For who hath despised the day of small things? For they shall rejoice, and shall see the plummet in the hand of Zerubabel with those seven. They are the eyes of the lord which run to and fro through the whole earth.*

*Zechariah 4:10*

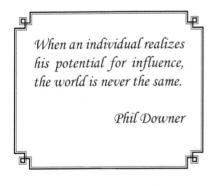

*When an individual realizes his potential for influence, the world is never the same.*

*Phil Downer*

It is the indefatigable law of growth and change that sustains every lively venture. If something is not growing, then it is not glowing. Nothing ever starts big at the beginning; rather, it starts small and grows big. The journey of one thousand kilometers, they say, starts just with a step. The days of little beginning are the most important days in any successful venture. On such days, you make all the mistakes permissible or not permissible without the media blowing it up.

You learn all you've got to learn and plan a foundation capable of carrying your dream tower. No one who despises his minor abilities ever excels in life; you must count on what you have before you bank on what you expect. What you need to start any world-class enterprise, I have found out, is available to even the poorest farmer in any village: *sitting down*. It sounds so simple. To sit down means to plan, to figure the cost of a project and design it. It is the most important aspect of life in your life (see Luke 14:28).

When you understand how significant the insignificant opportunities you now have are, you will definitely be surprised. The level of your accomplishment in the nearest future may be dependent on the little steps you are ignoring at the moment. You can make a difference with just the little opportunity, privilege, time, position, or talent you have at the moment. The problem is not your location or accommodation, but your conviction. Learn to bloom where you are planted, and make a difference in your life and in the lives of others.

## Starfish to Stardom

A man walking along a beach was surprised to observe a young man running toward the water. He watched the man toss something into the sea, run back across the sand, pick up something, and then sprint toward the water again and throw the object beyond the point where the waves were breaking.

"What are you doing?" the man inquired.

"I'm saving starfish by throwing them back into the sea," the young man replied. "The sun is coming up, and the tide is going out. If I don't act quickly, they all will die."

The man chuckled at what he perceived as a futile effort. "But there are miles of beach and many thousands of starfish lying on them right now; you can't possibly get to them all. What difference can you make?"

After listening politely, the young man bent over, picked up another starfish, ran toward the water, and gently tossed it beyond the incoming waves. Turning to the man, he answered, "I make a difference for that one."

The above story illustrates the call of God on each and every one of us. We need not change the whole world in one sweep, but individually, by playing our parts with commitment and dedication, we can make many differences rather than just one difference.

You are either a liberator or a liability. With the little you have, God expects you to embark on a liberation venture. Ask yourself, "Am I making a difference with what I am doing?" "Am I solving a problem or contributing to problems?" Success will remain elusive to the man who has no plan to change the world around him. There can be no true success until we succeed in doing the Master's job. Touching lives with what God gave us freely as talents, gifts, and privileges is the only key that will open the door of greater breakthrough in your life.

It is the seed you sow in people's lives that will germinate into your prominence tomorrow. Being extraordinary means doing little things in extraordinary ways. When men are growing in selfishness, there is a call at the moment on you and me to make a difference in the lives of people around us. Bear in mind that every breakthrough in your life is a sign that you have broken into another assignment in life. Your wealth of knowledge, skills, talents, and money is the raw material you need to accomplish the purpose of God on earth. You will soon leave this earth, but you can be remembered not by the houses you built or the numerous wives, cars, and chieftaincy titles you covetously gathered to yourself, but by how many lives you touched.

Who knows how many hurting people have been praying and asking God to remember them? You never can tell why God allowed you the wonderful privileges you are enjoying at the moment. We are on assignment. Whether big or small, rich or poor, we have a part to play to affect our world. We cannot achieve fulfillment in ourselves until we learn to put fulfillment in the lives of others.

One day, I was surprisingly launched into a very strange world of depression. It was strange because I rarely get depressed. I tried to pray it out, but it was to no avail. I made up my mind to ignore the feeling, but it was a futile attempt. Then I began to wonder what had gone wrong with me. Little did I know that the devil was prying on my peace. Straight away, the Holy Spirit directed me to my saved mail, and I pulled out a bundle of letters written to me by people God has enabled me to touch over all my years as a minister and motivational and inspirational speaker. By the time I had read through only two out of the whole bunch, I couldn't help but start smiling. My countenance changed. My face shone with radiance. I felt as though I were on top of the world. I even forgot that I had been depressed a few minutes before. Some of the down moments in your life are yelling for attention through the lives you have attended to. Note that you can make a difference where you are now and in the life of that person with you now! Do it now!

# Chapter 21

## Integrity: Your Cornerstone to Greatness

*Let integrity and uprightness preserve me, for I wait on thee.*

*Psalm 25:21*

> *The degree to which you stand firm in your convictions and beliefs, and assume responsibility for what you say and do, determines your level of integrity.*

The *Funk and Wagnalls New Encyclopedia* defines integrity as "Uprightness of character, soundness; and undivided or unbroken state." Nothing preserves, protects, and promotes like integrity. Without integrity, a man is but a clown clothed in decaying flesh. Success is achieved through hard work, popularity is attained through charisma, and victory is won through sound strategy; but it is only integrity that can keep these successes and preserve them. (My previous book, *Pathway to Uncommon Success*, aptly explains this.) As the late preacher B. A. Idahosa stated, "Charisma will take you up there but it is only integrity that will keep up there."

The Chinese taught their children and wards strength. They imbibed in them the attitude of steadfastness, watchfulness in combat, and readiness and handling of both offensive and defensive weapons; but they forgot to instill in them the virtues of integrity. The Great Wall of China was historically known as a strong barrier against all forms of enemy attacks. For several decades, the walls remained impenetrable, and the inhabitants remained unconquerable.

However, after a while, a new generation of young Chinese emerged full of strength but bereft of integrity. They were sound in strategy and war planning but lacking in integrity. They trained for wars and battles but failed in morality. Unfortunately, the previously impenetrable wall was overthrown and broken down. The indomitable inhabitants became a subdued generation because of their lack of integrity. Immorality, a lack of discipline, and compromise with the enemy will bring a man to the dust. These things brought about the fall of the Great Wall.

The Chinese had the integrity of walls around their nation, but they had no integrity around their lives. When the enemy got through to their lives, the formidable physical integrity had to fall to the invading Mongolians. (That is history, but we learned from it.)

Your integrity ultimately dictates how effective you are as a parent, leader, business owner, employee, spouse, mentor, or anything else. Your integrity dictates the measure of true success that you achieve.

## Stand for What You Believe in

How strong do you stand by your beliefs and condition? How much do you believe in the call of God upon your life and your talents? Do you waver back and forth from one decision or behavior pattern to another? Do you stand firm with what you know to be right? Is your belief in what God has called you to do so strong that you won't let anyone or anything get in the way of your God-ordained purpose?

## Integrity and Decision Making

Every time you make a decision that lacks integrity, you experience increased temptation to relinquish responsibility for that decision, looking for whom to lay the blame upon. It's human nature not to want to take responsibility for decisions or actions we know are morally wrong. But we can avoid making the wrong decision by following the steps outlined below.

## Integrity Commandments for Winning Decisions

1. Control impulsiveness. Never make a permanent decision about a temporary situation.
2. Be aware of blind spots. Make sure that your emotions are not driving your decisions toward destruction.
3. Delegate with confidence. Surround yourself with people who are wise and competent. Empower them to perform, and do not become intimidated by their expertise.
4. Consider all the options and accept responsibility for your final decision. Stop, look, and listen for wise counsel, but always sift it through your own heart before making final conclusions. Pray for guidance.
5. Never go to war where there are no spoils. Choose your battles wisely, and make sure that what you fight for is worth your pay.
6. Be accurately informed. Make sure that you have all available facts before acting. Conjecture will inevitably lead you to crisis.
7. Contemplate the consequences. Consider all options and their possible results before taking action on any of them.

8. Take calculated risks. Do not allow your expectations to exceed the practical potentials and realities of your resources. Hope for the best possible outcome or solution but be prepared for a loss.
9. Be cost effective with time. If the return is not greater than the investment, then the endeavor is not worth your time.
10. Survive in order to thrive. "Allow yourself a 10 percent ratio to be wrong, a 50 percent likelihood of betrayal, and a 100 percent commitment to survive it all" (T. D. Jakes, *Maximize the Moment*).

Following these ten commandants above and employing them in your decision-making situations will save you the horrors of regret, blame, and disappointment. Both integrity and wisdom are important qualities that a high-flier must possess if he is to make an extraordinary impact. Your integrity shows you have the wisdom to develop your values and beliefs and the strength to act on them. As a result, you are likely to have great peace of mind no matter what anyone thinks about you actions. "If any of you lacks wisdom, let him ask of God, who gives to all liberally and without reproach, and it will be given to him" (James 1:5 NKJV). "Therefore in all thy getting, get integrity with it also get wisdom which is the principal thing" (Proverbs 4:7).

# Chapter 22

## The Power of a Paradigm Shift

*Then said I, Ah Lord God: behold I cannot speak for I am a child.*

*Jeremiah 1:6*

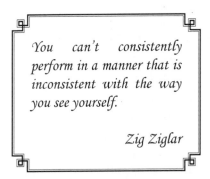

*You can't consistently perform in a manner that is inconsistent with the way you see yourself.*

*Zig Ziglar*

The best way to bring focus into your life is never to place a question mark where God has put a period. Distraction is the outstanding enemy of a purposeful life; it is evidence of confusion and imitation. You are complete in your makeup; nothing is actually lacking in you, right from the onset. The more than six billion brain cells you possess are more than enough to put you on the fast lane to an elevated pedestal. But the problem has always been our perspectives toward the things around us and the things that happen to us and within us.

## What Is a Paradigm?

The word "paradigm" comes from the Greek. It was originally a scientific term and is most commonly used today to mean "a model, theory, perception, assumption, or frame of reference." In a more general sense, it's the way we see the world—not in terms of our visual sense of sight, but in terms of perceiving, understanding, and interpreting.

Paradigms are maps—direction charts. A map is not a territory; a map is simply an explanation of certain aspects of the territory depicted on it. A paradigm can be said to be a theory, an explanation, or a model of something else.

## Change of Paradigm—Change of Pursuit

Most men exchange their lifetime for mediocrity, pursuing the wind of life. The busyness of our world has rendered people active yet unproductive. Some are basking in the anesthesia of hard work thinking that they are self-responsible. The truth remains that every one of us is performing in consonance with the way we each see things. Most of us are short-changing ourselves by pursuing things we know we are not gifted, equipped, or called to pursue. Because of challenges, self, or egoistic pressure, we dabble in battles not meant for us, thus messing ourselves up. Let us assume you are on a journey to arrive at a specific location—say London, Canada. A road map of the city would be a great asset to help you in reaching your destination. But suppose you were given the wrong map. Through the "printer's devil" an error occurred, and the map is labeled "London, United Kingdom" but the map is actually that of London, Ontario, Canada. Now can you imagine the frustration, the futility, of trying to reach your destination?

Here is a take-home assignment for you. Now get ready. Sit down in a quiet place, just you and you alone. Now take stock of your life right from the beginning. Try to find out where your life is heading. Do you feel a sense of fulfillment? Do you have confidence that you are getting to your purpose in life?

Do you take pleasure in the sacrifice you are making now to actualize your life vision? Without being motivated, encouraged, and rewarded, do you think you are internally motivated enough to pursue that goal? Try to find answers to these posers. Your answer will determine whether you are rightly positioned for excellence in life; otherwise, you need a paradigm change.

## Understanding a Paradigm Change

I was taught in an executive management class that "change is the challenge of management." When we refuse to read the signals and make the necessary adjustments, we are like a ship approaching a lighthouse with the captain of the ship demanding that the lighthouse should adjust its sail to avoid collision. This sounds funny because lighthouses are buildings stationed to direct sailors; they are never moving bodies like ships.

Our calling, purpose, or divine callings never change, but we do. The degree of deviation from our purpose in life affects the extent of our success and fulfillment in life. In order for us to achieve success, we have to make the right choice for the right change.

Let's remind ourselves again about the journey to London, Ontario, with the map wrongly labeled London, United Kingdom. There are obviously changes that must be carried out if you are to get to London, Ontario—your port of call. Behavioral and attitudinal changes cannot get you to London, Ontario; that is to say, no matter how hard you try to assume, point, confess by faith, and smile, you still won't get to the right place. Your attitude and behavior might be so positive that you are happy along the journey as you speed along in top gear, but the point is, you'll still be lost. The fundamental problem has everything to do with having a wrong map. If you have the right map of London, Ontario, then diligence becomes important, and when you encounter frustration along the way, your attitude can make a real difference. But the first and most important requirement is the accuracy of the map.

Each of us has many, many maps in our head, and they can be divided into two main categories: maps of the way things are, or realities, and maps of the way things should be, or values. We interpret everything we experience through these mental maps. We seldom question their accuracy; we are usually even unaware that we have them. We simply assume that the way we see things is the way they really are or the way they should be. And our attitude and behavior grow out of those assumptions. The way we see things is the source of the way we think and the way we act. Our actions are thus offshoots of our thoughts. This makes it difficult to achieve real success in life though the wrong paradigm. You may get there, but you won't be comfortable. You may achieve success, but you will not retain success. No amount of effort in the wrong direction will lead you to the right position.

Regarding paradigm change, we must be aware that our life is a function of the sum total of choices and decisions we make. Our decisions shows up in our actions, our actions precede our character, and our character gives birth to our habits. These habits, when formed, are harvested in our destiny. What color your life will be tomorrow is a function of the paradigm change you choose to make today. Do not be deceived; life is a function of choice and not chance. Luck is actually where opportunity and the right paradigm meet. In becoming extraordinary, you must make the right paradigm change.

# Chapter 23

## Live a Principle-Centered Life

*He is the Rock, his work is perfect: for all his ways are perfect: a God of truth and without iniquity just and right is he.*

*Deuteronomy 32:4*

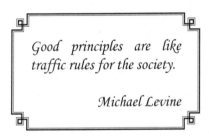

*Good principles are like traffic rules for the society.*

*Michael Levine*

Each of us has a center, though we usually don't recognize it as such. Neither do we recognize the all-encompassing effect of that center on every aspect of our lives. Most often, the life we live is composed of scripts handled over to us by our family, associates, other people's agendas, and the pressures of circumstance—scripts from our earlier years, from our training or our conditioning.

These scripts come from people, not principles. And they rise out of our deep vulnerabilities, our deep dependency on others, and our needs for acceptance and love, for belonging, for a sense of importance and worth, and for a feeling that we matter.

Whether we are aware of it or not, whether we are in control or not, there is a first creation in every part of our lives. We are either the second creation of our own proactive design, or we are the second creation of other people's agendas, of circumstances, or of past habits. We choose to remain in our initial created state without development, just watching events as they come and go. Or we can choose to rewrite our own life script upon some basic fundamental principles based on infallible standards of God.

## Living Your Script

There are so many ineffective principles, or scripts, we are living. These scripts can only be discovered when we embark on developing our own self-awareness. These ineffective scripts are deeply embedded habits that are totally unworthy of us, totally incongruent with the things we really value in life. Re-creating yourself now means being responsible enough to use your imagination and creativity to write new scripts that are more effective, and more congruent with, your deepest values and the correct principles that give our values meaning.

Your values determine what your principles are. The things you do reflect exactly what principle you live out. It is in the face of a crucial choice that we manifest the values we esteem in our lives. Your values, which produce your life principles, determine your center. Your center is that inalienable object of dependence without which your whole life would become uncoordinated. What you value, you esteem. What you esteem, you protect. What you protect is the center of your life.

## Your Principle Now Is Your Epitaph Then

The best way to bring focus to your life is to live out your epitaph now. I was in a meeting, and as the preacher began to preach, he paused and asked everyone in the audience to write down his or her personal mission statement. We all did exactly that. Then he went further to instruct us to type it and fasten it in a place where we could read it every morning. Then he gave us the shocker: "What you have on those pieces of papers are your epitaphs," he thundered. "Go and live your scripts!"

I have not forgotten the impact that short but powerful message had on me. Over time, I have worked, developed, and redeveloped my own personal mission statement. Having considered my call, and the scope of it, I have prayerfully committed myself to a vision bigger than my life itself. But I have made up my mind to live out my script and not some other person's script.

## Your Mission Statement Should Be Your Constitution

You could call a personal mission statement a personal constitution. I have a personal respect for the US Constitution. It's fundamentally changeless. In over two hundred years, there have been only twenty-six amendments, ten of which were in the original Bill of Rights. The US Constitution is the standard by which every law in the country is evaluated. It is the document every US president agrees to defend and support when he takes the oath of office. It is the criterion by which people are admitted into citizenship. It is the foundation and the center that enables people to ride through such traumas as the American Civil War or the destruction of the World Trade Center (WTC). It is the written standard, the criterion by which everything else is evaluated and directed.

The Constitution has endured and serves its vital function today because it is based on correct principles, on the self-evident truths contained in the Declaration of Independence. These principles empower the constitution with a timeless strength, even in the midst of social ambiguity and change. It was Thomas Jefferson who once said, "Our peculiar security is in the possession of a written constitution." A personal mission statement based on correct principle becomes the same kind of standard for an individual. It becomes a personal constitution, the basis for making major decisions in the midst of the circumstances and emotions that affect our lives. It empowers individuals with the same timeless strength in the midst of change.

It is important to note that people can't live or change if there's not a changeless cure inside them. Stephen R. Covey wrote in his wildly successful book *The Seven Habits of Highly Effective People,* "The key to the ability to change is a changeless sense of who you are, what you are about and what you value."

With a mission statement, we can flow with changes. We don't need prejudices or prejudgments. We don't need to figure out everything else in life. Once you have that sense of mission, you have the essence of your own actions or proactivity. You have the vision and values that direct life. You have the basic direction from which you set your long- and short-term goals. You have the power of a written constitution based on correct principles against which every decision concerning the most effective use of your talents and your energies can be measured.

Principles are deep fundamental truths—classic truths, not just facts. They are tightly interwoven threads running with exactness, consistency, and strength through the fabrics of our lives. Even in the midst of people or circumstances, we can be assured by the knowledge that principles are bigger than people or circumstances, and that thousands of years of history have seen them triumph time and time again. Be principled; be extraordinary!

# Chapter 24

## *Become Proactive*

*Brethren I count not myself to have apprehended, but this one thing I do, forgetting those things which are behind, and reaching forth unto those things which are before. I press toward the mark for the prize of the calling of God in Christ Jesus.*

*Philippians 3:13–14*

> *While one person hesitates because he feels inferior, the other is busy making mistakes [becoming proactive] and becoming superior.*
>
> *Henry C. Link*

Proactive men established every kingdom that existed on planet earth. You don't overthrow a tyrant through negotiations or peace accords. Revolution—or call it the force of revolution—must be applied. You must understand the importance of proactivity.

Every revolution, whether in an individual's life, community, or nation, is traceable to a revelation. Revelations are products of information. Until the right and relevant information is acquired, status quo ante will persist.

## Proactivity Defined

The word "proactivity" is now fairly common in management literature, though it is a word you won't find in most dictionaries. It means more than merely taking initiative. It means that as human beings, we are responsible for our own lives. Our behavior is a function of our decisions, not our conditions. We can subordinate feelings to values. We have the initiative and the responsibility to make things happen.

Responsibility simply means "response ability," that is, the ability to choose your response. Highly proactive people recognize that in being responsible, they do not blame circumstances, conditions, or conditioning for their behavior. Their behavior is a product of their own conscious choice; it is based on values rather than a product of their conditions based on feeling.

Because we are, by nature, proactive, if our lives are a function of conditioning and conditions, it is because we have, by conscious decision or by default, chosen to empower those things to control us. In making such a choice, we become proactive.

Reactive people are often affected by their physical environment. Their physical environment often affects them. If the weather is good, they feel good; if it isn't, it affects their attitude and their performance. Proactive people can carry their own weather with them. Whether it rains or shines makes no difference to them. They are value driven, and their commitment to produce good-quality work isn't a function of whether their environment is conducive to it or not.

The ability to subordinate an impulse to a value is the essence of the productive person. Reactive people are driven by feelings, by circumstances, by conditions, by their environment. Proactive people are driven by values—carefully thought-about, selected, and internalized values. Proactive people are still influenced by external stimuli, whether physical, social, or psychological; but their response to stimuli, conscious or unconscious, is a value-based choice or response.

It was Eleanor Roosevelt who once stated, "No one can hurt you without your consent." In the same respect, if we do not give in to them, it is our willing permission, our consent to what happens to us, that hurts us far more than what happens to us in the first place.

Being proactive is simply being a risk taker. Proactive people understand that without risk there will be no rise. Allow me to tell you the story of someone who pushed the envelope of risk in order to achieve the goals that were valuable to her.

Amelia Earhart, simply called Millie, was born in Kansas, USA, in 1897. She was bright and excelled academically. She liked reading books and reciting poetry. She also enjoyed sports, particularly basketball and tennis.

After recognizing the impact of war on the soldiers who served in Europe during World War I, Millie wanted to do something to help. She decided to study nursing, and during the war, she worked as a military nurse's aide in Canada. After the war was over, she enrolled as a premed student at Columbia University in New York. In 1920, after her first year at school was finished, she visited her family in Los Angeles. That's when she took her first plane ride at Daugherty Field in Long Beach, California. And she was hooked. "As soon as we left the ground I knew I myself had to fly," she said. She never returned to medical school.

That was the beginning of a proactive life for Millie. I should mention that Millie immediately began working odd jobs to earn the $1,000 required to take flying lessons, and soon she was learning how to fly from another pioneer and proactive flier called Anita Snook.

Learning how to fly was not easy for her; she had more than her share of crashes, yet she persevered. Years later, she told her husband her perspective on flying: "Please know I am quite aware of the hazards . . . I want to do it because I want to do it. Women must try to do things as men have tried. When they fail, their failure must be but a challenge to others." What a proactive statement!

## The Woman with Many Records

During the course of her flying career, Earhart set many records and achieved many firsts:

1. 1928: First woman to cross the Atlantic Ocean in an aircraft as passenger
2. 1929: First president of the Ninety-Nines, an association of female pilots
3. 1930: Women's speed record of 181.8 miles per hour on a three-kilometer course
4. 1931: First person to set an altitude record in an early helicopter at 18,451 feet
5. 1932: First female pilot to fly solo over the Atlantic
6. 1935: First person to fly solo and nonstop between Oakland, California, and Honolulu, Hawaii

Now it is your turn. "If at first you do succeed, try something harder" (John Maxwell).

# Chapter 25

## Determine to Make a Difference

*So David conquered the Philistine giant with a sling and a stone. Since he had no sword, he ran over and pulled Goliath's from its sheath and killed him with it and then cut off his head. When the Philistines saw that there champion was dead, they turned and ran.*

*1 Samuel 17:50, 51 (TLB)*

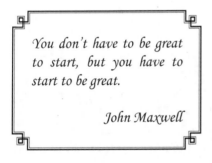

*You don't have to be great to start, but you have to start to be great.*

*John Maxwell*

Determination simply means the termination of a terminal tension. Every obstacle before you is but a tension to you. Tensions are challenges that can easily destabilize a man and subsequently defeat him. Your ability to confront and overwhelm such tension brings about the opportunity to really make a difference in your life and the lives of others. Many people want to wait for inspiration before they are willing to step out and take a risk. I find that is especially true of people with an artistic bent, who look at issues cosmetically.

## Enough Risks to Make a Difference

Risks are necessary for any worthwhile venture. Taking enough risks guarantees you will have enough opportunities to make a difference. If you follow where the paths lead instead of blazing your own trail and beating your own pathway, you will remain a mediocrity all your life.

As you examine the way you live, consider whether you are taking enough risks—not senseless ones, but intelligent ones. Be informed. If you are succeeding in everything you do, then you're probably not pushing yourself hard enough. And that means you're not taking enough risks to guarantee your making a difference.

## Another Risk-Taker with a Difference

The story of Amelia Earhart may not appeal to your sense of security or masculine chauvinism. However, the risks people like her take may seem too different from your life situation for you to connect with them. If so, now read through the life of someone whose quiet willingness to take risks may seem more like your own:

Joseph Lister was a second-generation physician born in England in 1827. Back in the days when he began practicing medicine, surgery was a painful, grisly affair. If you had the misfortune of being injured and requiring surgery in the mid-1800s, here's what you could have expected: You would have been taken to a hospital's surgical theater, a building that was separate from the main hospital to prevent the regular patients from becoming upset by the screaming. (Anesthesia had not yet been developed then, mind you.) You would have been strapped to a table that looked a lot like the one in your kitchen, under which sat a tub of sand, positioned to catch blood.

Your surgery would have been performed by a physician or barber likely surrounded by a group of observers and assistants. All of them would be dressed in the regular street clothes they wore throughout the course of the day while traveling around town and treating patients. The instruments the doctor used would have been pulled from a nearby tray where they had been placed (unwashed) after the previous surgery. And if your surgeon needed his hands free while working on you, he might have held the surgical knife between his teeth.

Your chances of surviving surgery would be a little better than 50 percent. If you had the misfortune of having your operation in a military hospital, your chances of survival may go down to about 10 percent. Of surgery during that era, one contemporary doctor wrote, "A man laid on the operating table in one of our surgical hospitals is exposed to more chances of death than the English soldier on the field of Waterloo."

## Determined to Make a Difference

Like the other surgeons of his time, Lister was distressed by the death rate of patients, but he was ignorant of the cause. However, he was determined to discover a way to save more of his patients.

Lister's first major breakthrough came after he was given some writing by his friend Thomas Anderson, a chemistry professor. Scientist Louis Pasteur wrote the papers. In them the French scientist stated his opinion that gangrene was caused not by air but by bacteria and germs present in air. Lister thought those ideas were remarkable. And he theorized that if the dangerous microbes could be eliminated, his patients would have a better chance of avoiding gangrene, blood poisoning, and the other infections that often killed them.

## His Innovation Made Him an Outcast

Every novel idea at first sounds foolish because it often seems out of order. Because of what we know today about germs and infections, Lister's ideas may seem to be common sense. But his belief was radical in those days—even among members of the medical community. And when Lister, who was working at a hospital in Edinburgh, presented his beliefs and findings to the senior surgeons, he was taunted, ridiculed, and rejected. Each day as he made his rounds, his colleagues insulted and criticized him. He was really an outcast. You can be an outcast, but don't let life cast you out of relevance.

## The Result—the Difference

In 1867, Lister published his findings, and still the medical profession ridiculed him. For more than a decade, he communicated his clinical findings and encouraged other doctors to adopt his practices. Finally in 1881, sixteen years after his first success with a patient, his peers at the International Medical Congress held in London recognized his advances. They called his works perhaps the greatest advances that surgery had ever made. In 1883, he was knighted. In 1897, he was made a baron.

Today, if you've had any kind of surgery, or if you are a member of the medical profession like myself, you owe Dr. Joseph Lister a debt of gratitude. His risks secured our safety, and he is still making a difference in the lives of many millions who survive major surgeries today (culled from *Motivated to Succeed* by John C. Maxwell).

# Chapter 26

## Take a Risk: There's No Other Way to Be Extraordinary

*But without faith it is impossible to please Him. For he that cometh to God must believe that He is and He is a rewarder of them that diligently seek Him.*

*Hebrews 11:6*

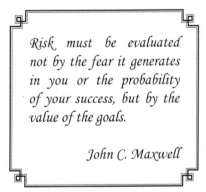

*Risk must be evaluated not by the fear it generates in you or the probability of your success, but by the value of the goals.*

*John C. Maxwell*

In life, there are no safe places or risk-free demilitarized zones. Helen Keller, author, speaker, and advocate for disabled persons, asserted that "security is mostly a superstition. It does not exist in nature, nor do the children of men as a whole experience it. Avoiding danger is no safer in the long run than outright exposure. Life is either a daring adventure or nothing."

Everything in life brings risk. It's true that you risk failure if you try something bold, because you might miss the mark. But you also risk failure if you stand still and don't try anything new. G. K. Chesterton wrote, "I do not believe in a fate that falls on men however they act; but I do believe in a fate that falls on them unless they act." The less you venture out, the greater your risks of failure. Ironically, the more you risk failure—and the more you actually fail—the greater your chances of success.

When it comes to taking risks, I believe there are two kinds of people: those who don't dare try new things, and those who don't dare miss them. Let's look at the characteristics of these two categories of people.

UNDARING PEOPLE

1. They resist opportunities.
2. They rationalize their responsibilities.
3. They keep rehearing impossibilities.
4. They envy enthusiasm.
5. They keep reviewing their inadequacies.
6. They recoil at the failure of others.
7. They often reject the personal cost involved.
8. They replace goals with pleasure.
9. They rejoice that they have not failed.

DARING PEOPLE

1. They find opportunities.
2. They finish their responsibilities and business.
3. They feed on impossibilities.
4. They fan the flame of enthusiasm.
5. They face their inadequacies squarely.
6. They figure out why others failed and try to avoid the pitfalls.
7. They finance cost into their lifestyle in any venture.
8. They find pleasure in the goal.
9. They fear futility, not failure.

| | |
|---|---|
| 10. They rest before they finish. | 10. They finish before they rest. |
| 11. They resist leadership. | 11. They follow leaders. |
| 12. They remain unchanged. | 12. They force change to happen. |
| 13. They replay problems. | 13. They fish for solutions. |
| 14. They rethink their commitment. | 14. They fulfill their commitment. |
| 15. They reverse their decisions. | 15. They finalize their decisions. |

From the above list, it is obvious that belonging to the undaring category automatically qualifies you for a life of mediocrity. The motto of the mediocre is, "I would rather try nothing great and succeed than try something great and risk failure." On the other hand, if you classify yourself in the daring category, you are on your way to becoming extraordinary. The extraordinary people's motto is, "I would rather try something great and fail than try nothing great and succeed." The basic truth is that if you want to increase your odds of success, you have to take chances.

The willingness to take greater risks is a major key to achieving success. You may be surprised that it can solve two very different kinds of problems. First, if you've been hitting all the goals you set for yourself, then you need to increase your willingness to take chances. The road to the next level is always uphill, so you can't coast there. You must be constantly moving up against all resisting forces. When you slow down, you are on your way downward.

On the other hand, if you find yourself in a place where it seems that you don't achieve many of your goals, you may be playing it too safe. You must never forget that the answer to getting to the level of your life lies in your willingness to take even greater risks.

It was the late Papa Benson Idahosa who said, "It is risky not to take risk, and if you don't take chances, you will never make advances." Even having faith in God is a risky venture. Any act of faith is always an act of risk. It takes a completely committed risk-taker to walk by faith.

Barely a year after I graduated from my university, when most of my colleagues were still in their parents' houses, eating their parents' food and wearing clothing their parents bought them, I veered into an independent life. It wasn't easy, but I refused to be dependent on anybody. Not much later, I took a huge leap and bought a car. I didn't have the money, but I risked my way into buying that car. It may surprise you to know that God honored that risk and pushed the money to me instantly. The car was not a showy one, but it was a necessity for my next level. Are you ready for the next level? Then get ready to risk your current comfort zone.

# Action Plan

## *Confession of Faith*

*A man's belly shall be satisfied with the fruit of his mouth, and with the increase of his lips shall he be filled. Death and life [promotion, prosperity, success, extraordinary] are in the power of the tongue: and they that love it shall eat the fruit thereof.*

*Proverbs 18:20–21*

There is power in the spoken word. In the spiritual realm, words are the only raw materials for creating things in the physical world. Your angels are idle because you do not know how to use them to bring your demands into reality. Your wish is their command. However, they act only on the Word. So start speaking into existence your wishes according to the Word. Never relent until they are manifested.

"But to which of the angels said he at any time, sit on my right hand, until I make thine enemies thy footstool? Are they not all ministering spirits, sent fort to minister for them who shall be heirs of salvation?" (Hebrews 1:13–14). Child of God, did you hear that? These special creatures are specially designed to minister *for* you. Here the word "minister" means "to serve, assist, help, work for, and provide for." I challenge you to hold on to your positive confessions according to the Word and liberate yourself from being just important to being an extraordinary person. You can travel with me as we make the following power-packed confessions. I want you to believe God for a new mentality that will bring about your prosperity. Get ready now! Your angels are waiting to act.

Now pray these confessions loud for the hearing of both the devil and your angels:

> *I am born again, regenerated, and re-created by God (see 2*
>     *Corinthians 5:17).*
> *I have passed from death to life (see Romans 8:1–2).*
> *I am of strange value.*
> *I am carrying a new gene that is coded the same as God's.*
> *I am peculiar to deliver peculiar results.*
> *I reject mediocrity; that is not where I belong.*
> *I can't be ordinary, though I was ordinary before I met*
>     *Christ.*
> *God sent Jesus as a star, and Jesus sent me as a star.*
> *I am to be envied, not pitied.*
> *I am relevant to this generation. I am a liberator, not a*
>     *liability.*
> *I have what it takes to be a star. It is not a balloon*
>     *prophesy (see Daniel 12:13).*
> *Wisdom, the force behind the star in the kingdom, is my*
>     *new creation right.*
> *I have the mind of Christ (see 1 Corinthians 2:16).*
> *I have what it takes to be a star; I cannot afford to*
>     *disappoint re-creation.*
> *The mind I have is the mind of God (see Proverbs 3:19, 1*
>     *Corinthians 2:16).*
> *I carry the virtue of creation; therefore, I am to create*
>     *things.*
> *I am born into a world of limitless opportunities. I cannot*
>     *afford to live ordinarily.*
> *I refuse to be down, because there is a place for me at the*
>     *top.*

*I am extraordinarily re-created to make extraordinary*
*impacts.*
*I am blood-bought, heaven-sanctified. I bear the mark of*
*redemption.*
*The top is my place, and I will never miss my position.*

Now listen to this:

The world is waiting for you. You are duty bound to deliver because it took God His life to give you the mind, power, and privileges you have now. You have what it takes to be extraordinary. You are carrying the force that created the whole world; don't you think you can re-create the world around you the way you want it? It is time for your star to rise. You cannot afford to suffer frustration anymore. Arise and shine, for your light has come and the glory of the Lord has risen upon you in Jesus's name.

Dare to be extraordinary!